QUILTING
Through the Year
with Debbie Mumm®

The first buds of springtime ... The warm weather delights of summer ...
The beautiful colors of autumn ... The reflection of sunshine on snow ...
Celebrate each season with beautiful quilting projects to enjoy all through the year!

Dear Friends,

I love the changing seasons ... the first buds of springtime, the warm-weather delights of summer, the beautiful colors of autumn, the reflection of sunshine on the snow ... and I love to celebrate these seasonal changes by introducing new quilt designs and accents into my home décor.

It's remarkable how a few seasonal changes indoors can magnify the glorious changes happening outdoors to give my home and my spirit a fresh, new perspective.

In this book, we celebrate the changing of the seasons with quilting and home decorating projects to help you renew your home as nature transforms your surroundings. It is my hope that you'll use this book all through the year to add beautiful seasonal projects to every room.

We've included a wide variety of projects so that you'll find lots of inspirational ideas. Chicks and bunnies frolic across a sweet crib quilt in our spring chapter and the gorgeous Hearts and Flowers quilt would be perfect for a wedding or anniversary celebration. We celebrate summer with a grouping of quilts that practically shout SUMMER FUN! From a paper-pieced lighthouse to a handsome cabin quilt, from patriotic pinwheels to projects made with beach and forest finds, you'll discover lots of projects to bring the outdoors inside.

Pumpkins, leaves, cornstalks, and even a quail bring the colors and symbols of autumn to our fall sewing projects. From two versatile quilt patterns you can make four projects! Top off your autumn accents with our easy centerpiece painting project. You'll be warm and cozy all winter with our easy flannel quilt or celebrate the season with the sensational Snow Crystals Lap Quilt.

All through the year you're sure to find lots of quilting projects and decorating accents for every season and every room. Enjoy a year full of quilting fun!

Your Friend,

Debbie Mumm

Table of Contents

Finished Size: 90½" x 116"

Hearts and Flowers
B e d   Q u i l t

A brilliant bouquet of flowers blooms on this beautiful bed quilt that is perfect for a "heart-warming" present or a spring update for your bedroom. Brightly hued sprays of heart-centered blooms send an unmistakable message of springtime joy, while our quick-piecing methods ensure speedy completion.

Fabric Requirements and Cutting Instructions

Read all instructions before beginning and use ¼"-wide seam allowances throughout. Read Cutting the Strips and Pieces on page 78 prior to cutting fabrics.

Hearts and Flowers Bed Quilt 90½" x 116"	FIRST CUT		SECOND CUT	
	Number of Strips or Pieces	Dimensions	Number of Pieces	Dimensions
Fabric A Background 5¾ yards	3	26¾" x 42"	3	26¾" squares**
	1	13⅝" x 42"	2	13⅝" squares*
	16	4½" x 42"	12	4½" x 18½"
			12	4½" x 10½"
			48	4½" squares
	8	2½" x 42"	120	2½" squares
	8	1½" x 42"	192	1½" squares
Fabric B Large Heart Light Petals ½ yard each of four fabrics	2	4½" x 42"	12	4½" x 5½"
	1	2½" x 42"	6	2½" squares
	1	1½" x 42"	24	1½" squares
	cut for each of four fabrics			
Fabric C Large Heart Dark Petals ½ yard each of four fabrics	2	4½" x 42"	12	4½" x 5½"
	1	2½" x 42"	6	2½" squares
	1	1½" x 42"	24	1½" squares
	cut for each of four fabrics			
Fabric D Small Heart Dark Petals ¼ yard each of six fabrics	2	3½" x 42"	6	3½" squares
			12	3½" x 2½"
	cut for each of six fabrics; you'll have a few pieces left over			
Fabric E Small Heart Light Petals ¼ yard each of six fabrics	2	3½" x 42"	6	3½" squares
			12	3½" x 2½"
	cut for each of six fabrics; you'll have a few pieces left over			
BORDERS				
First Border ½ yard	10	1½" x 42"		
Second Border ⅜ yard	10	1" x 42"		
Outside Border 1⅝ yards	10	5½" x 42"		
Binding 1 yard	11	2¾" x 42"		
Backing - 8½ yards Batting - 100" x 125"				

**cut twice diagonally for side-setting triangles*
cut once diagonally for corner-setting triangles

Making the Blocks

You'll be making twelve Large Heart Petal Blocks and six Small Heart Petal Blocks. All blocks measure 18½" unfinished. Whenever possible, use the Assembly Line Method on page 78. Press in the direction of arrows.

Large Heart Petal Blocks

Directions are for one block. Refer to the block diagram below, the quilt layout on page 9, and the color photo to help with fabric placement as you work. Each block consists of light and dark fabric.

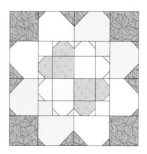

1. Refer to Quick Corner Triangles on page 78. Sew 1½" and 2½" Fabric A squares to 4½" x 5½" Fabric B piece as shown. Press. Sew 1½" and 2½" Fabric A squares to 4½" x 5½" Fabric C piece as shown. Press. Make two of each variation.

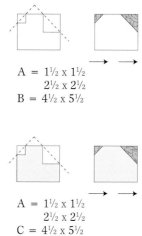

A = 1½ x 1½
   2½ x 2½
B = 4½ x 5½

A = 1½ x 1½
   2½ x 2½
C = 4½ x 5½
Make 2 of each variation

2. Repeat step 1 to sew 1½" and 2½" Fabric A squares to a matching 4½" x 5½" Fabric B piece as shown. Press. Sew 1½" and 2½" Fabric A squares to a matching 4½" x 5½" Fabric C piece. Press. Make two of each variation.

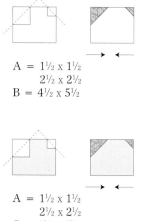

A = 1½ x 1½
    2½ x 2½
B = 4½ x 5½

A = 1½ x 1½
    2½ x 2½
C = 4½ x 5½
Make 2 of each variation

3. Making quick corner triangle units, sew two 1½" Fabric B squares to a 3½" x 2½" Fabric D piece as shown. Use the same Fabric B as used in step 2. Press. Make four identical units. Repeat step using two 1½" Fabric C squares and 3½" x 2½" Fabric E piece. Press. Make four of each variation.

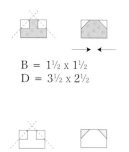

B = 1½ x 1½
D = 3½ x 2½

C = 1½ x 1½
E = 3½ x 2½
Make 4 of each variation

4. Sew 2½" Fabric B square to a matching unit from step 3 as shown. Press. Sew 2½" Fabric C square to a matching unit from step 3. Press. Make two of each variation.

2½

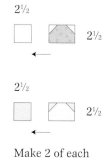
2½

2½

2½

Make 2 of each variation

5. Sew a matching 3½" Fabric D square to a unit from step 3 as shown. Press. Make two. Sew a matching 3½" Fabric E square to remaining units from step 3. Press. Make two of each variation.

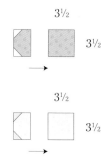
3½

3½

3½

3½

Make 2 of each variation

6. Sew matching units from step 4 and step 5 together as shown. Press. Make two of each variation.

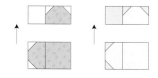

Make 2 of each variation

7. Sew a unit from step 2 to each matching unit from step 6 as shown. Press. Make two of each variation.

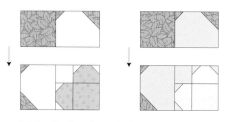

Make 2 of each variation

8. Sew 4½" Fabric A square to each unit from step 1 as shown. Press. Make two of each variation.

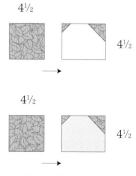
4½

4½

4½

4½

Make 2 of each variation

9. Sew a unit from step 8 to a matching-colored unit from step 7 as shown. Press. Make two of each variation.

Make 2 of each variation

10. Arrange units from step 9 in two rows as shown. Sew units into rows. Press. Sew rows together. Press seams in one direction. Block measures 18½" square.

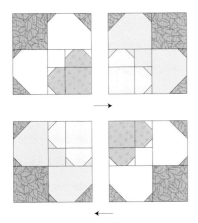

Block measures 18½" square

11. Repeat steps 1 through 10 to make twelve blocks.

Small Heart Petal Blocks

Directions are for one block. Each block includes two different shades of the same color. Refer to the block diagram below, the quilt layout on page 9, and the color photo on page 4 to help with fabric placement as you work. You'll have a few Fabric D and E pieces left over.

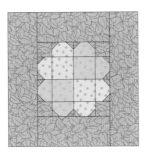

1. Refer to Large Heart Petal Blocks. Follow steps 3 through 6, on page 6, substituting 1½" and 2½" Fabric A squares for 1½" and 2½" Fabric B and C squares. Make four units for each block, two each using Fabrics A and D and two each using Fabrics A and E.

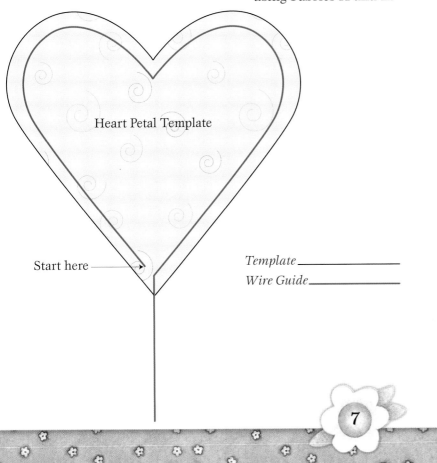

Heart Petal Template

Start here ⟶

Template _____

Wire Guide _____

Heart Flowers

Pretty heart-shaped petals form these dimensional flowers.

Fabric Requirements

For one flower
Flower (⅛ yard each of two fabrics)
Heavyweight fusible web (⅓ yard)
24-gauge wire - nine 20" lengths
Wire florist stem - one
Florist tape
Decorative button - one

Making One Flower

1. *Form 24-gauge wire into heart shape as shown in Heart Petal Template at left. Make eight.*

2. *Refer to Quick Fuse Appliqué on page 79 and Heart Petal Template. Trace sixteen heart petals onto paper side of fusible web. Fuse eight traced heart petals onto each Flower fabric. Cut out hearts.*

3. *Remove paper from two matching heart petals. Place one heart petal fusible side facing up, and place pre-formed wire on top.*

4. *With wire between, align two matching heart petals, fusible sides together.*

5. *Fuse heart petal in sections, being careful to keep wire in place and fabrics aligned. Press one side of heart petal, then other side. For best results, let fabric cool between pressing sections. Repeat to make eight heart petals.*

6. *Form one wire into a U shape, insert into holes of button, twisting wire behind.*

7. *Arrange button and four petals together, wrapping wire around florist stem.*

8. *Arrange remaining petals around unit from step 7, wrapping wires around stem. Wrap wires and stem with florist tape. Cut stem to desired length.*

9. *Repeat steps 1-8 to make additional flowers.*

2. Arrange units from step 1 in two rows as shown. Sew units into rows. Press. Sew rows together. Press.

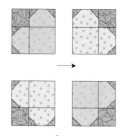

3. Sew unit from step 2 between two 4½" x 10½" Fabric A pieces. Press.

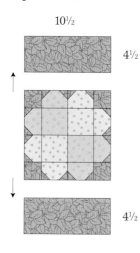

4. Sew unit from step 3 between two 4½" x 18½" Fabric A strips as shown. Press.

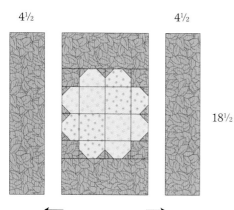

Block measures 18½" square

5. Repeat steps 1 through 4 to make six blocks.

Assembly

1. Quilt is assembled in diagonal rows. Arrange alternating Large Heart Petal and Small Heart Petal Blocks, 26¾" side-setting triangles, and 13⅝" corner-setting triangles as shown. (You'll have two side-setting triangles left over.) Sew blocks and triangles into rows. Press seams away from Large Heart Petal Blocks.

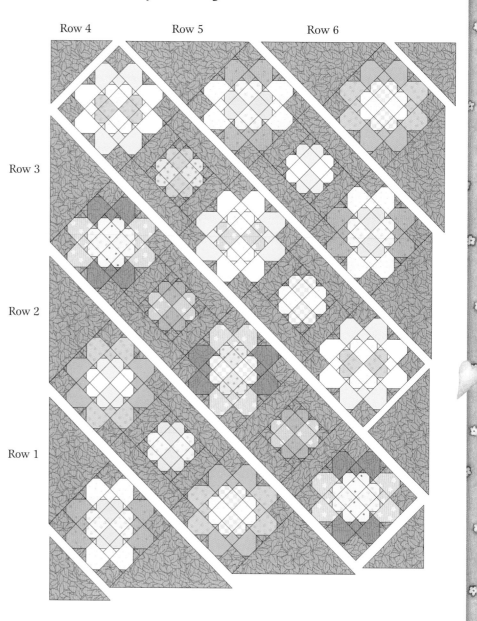

2. Sew rows together. Press seams in one direction. Finish by adding 13⅝" corner triangles. Press seams toward corner triangles. Trim quilt top edges as necessary, making sure to leave ¼" seam allowance on all sides.

Borders

1. Sew 1½"-wide First Border strips end to end to make one continuous 1½"-wide First Border strip. Press. Measure quilt through center from side to side. Trim two 1½"-wide First Border strips to that measurement. Sew to top and bottom of quilt. Press seams toward border.

2. Measure quilt through center from top to bottom, including borders just added. Trim two 1½"-wide First Border strips to that measurement. Sew to sides of quilt. Press.

3. Repeat steps 1 and 2 to join, fit, trim, and sew 1"-wide Second Border strips and 5½"-wide Outside Border strips to top, bottom, and sides of quilt.

Layering and Finishing

1. Cut backing crosswise into three equal pieces. Sew pieces together to make one 102" x 126" (approximate) backing piece. Arrange and baste backing, batting, and top together, referring to Layering the Quilt on page 80.

2. Hand or machine quilt as desired.

3. Sew 2¾"-wide binding strips end to end to make one continuous 2¾"-wide binding strip. Press. Refer to Binding the Quilt on page 80 and bind quilt to finish.

H e a r t s   a n d   F l o w e r s   B e d   Q u i l t

Finished Size: 90½" x 116"
Photo: page 4

Finished Size: 44" x 30"

Spring Blooms
Wall Quilt

Perky pieced tulips grow out of colorful flowerpots on this simply sensational wall quilt. Flowerpots use an easy appliqué technique and the broad borders show off pretty prints — perfect for bright colors and retro fabrics. This easy wall quilt can be the first sign of spring at your home!

WELCOME

Fabric Requirements and Cutting Instructions

Read all instructions before beginning and use 1/4"-wide seam allowances throughout. Read Cutting the Strips and Pieces on page 78 prior to cutting fabrics.

Spring Blooms Wall Quilt 44" x 30"	FIRST CUT	
	Number of Strips or Pieces	Dimensions
Fabric A Background *1/3 yard each of three fabrics*	1*	6" x 10½"
	1*	3" x 10½"
	6*	2½" squares
	2*	2" x 10½"
	2*	1½" x 5½"
Fabric B Leaves *1/8 yard each of three fabrics*	2*	2½" x 5½"
	2*	2½" squares
	1*	1½" x 4½"
Fabric C Flowers *scraps**	2*	2½" x 4½"
Fabric D Flower Pot Rim *scraps**	1*	3" x 8½"
Fabric E Flower Pot Base *scraps**	1*	6" x 6½"
BORDERS		
First Border *1/6 yard*	3	1½" x 42"
Second Border *1/4 yard*	3	2" x 42"
Outside Border *3/4 yard***	4	4½" x 42"
Binding *5/8 yard for bias* *3/8 yard for straight cut*		2¾" bias strips cut from 21" square
Backing - 1⅜ yards Batting - 48" x 34" Three 1" buttons *Cut for each of three fabrics **Extra fabric allowed for matching plaid*		

Making the Blocks

You will be making three blocks constructed with different fabrics for background, tulips, and flowerpots. The flowerpots are appliquéd on two sides to the background and then sewn to the remaining strips and units. To speed the piecing process, refer to quilt layout and arrange all fabrics by block. Unfinished block measures 10½" x 16½". Whenever possible use the Assembly Line Method on page 78. Press in the direction of arrows.

1. Refer to Quick Corner Triangles on page 78. Sew 2½" Fabric A square and 2½" Fabric B square to 2½" x 4½" Fabric C piece as shown. Press. Make three, one of each color variation.

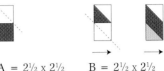

A = 2½ x 2½
C = 2½ x 4½

B = 2½ x 2½

Make 3
(1 of each variation)

2. Making quick corner triangle units, sew one 2½" Fabric A square and one 2½" Fabric B square to 2½" x 4½" Fabric C piece as shown. Press. Make three, one of each variation.

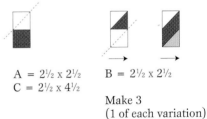

A = 2½ x 2½
C = 2½ x 4½

B = 2½ x 2½

Make 3
(1 of each variation)

3. Sew matching units from steps 1 and 2 together as shown. Press. Sew a matching 1½" x 4½" Fabric B piece to bottom of unit as shown. Make three, one of each variation. Press.

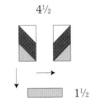

4½

1½

Make 3
(1 of each variation)

4. Making quick corner triangle units, sew two matching 2¹/₂" Fabric A squares to 2¹/₂" x 5¹/₂" Fabric B piece as shown. Press. Make three and three reversed, one of each variation.

A = 2¹/₂ x 2¹/₂
B = 2¹/₂ x 5¹/₂
Make 3
(1 of each variation)

A = 2¹/₂ x 2¹/₂
B = 2¹/₂ x 5¹/₂
Make 3
(1 of each variation)

5. Sew each unit from step 3 between matching units from step 4 as shown. Press. Make three, one of each variation.

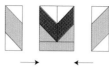

Make 3
(1 of each variation)

6. Sew each unit from step 5 between two matching 1¹/₂" x 5¹/₂" Fabric A pieces. Press. Make three, one of each variation.

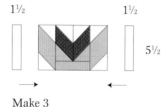

1¹/₂   1¹/₂

5¹/₂

Make 3
(1 of each variation)

7. Referring to Flowerpot Rim Template on page 13, trace and cut Fabric D using pattern. Turn under ¹/₄"-wide side seam allowances on flowerpot rim, center on 3" x 10¹/₂" Fabric A piece, and hand or machine appliqué (sides only) in place. Make three, one of each variation.

8. Referring to Flowerpot Base Template below, trace and cut Fabric E using pattern. Turn under ¹/₄"-wide side seam allowances on flowerpot, center on 6" x 10¹/₂" Fabric A piece, and hand or machine appliqué (sides only) in place. Make three, one of each variation.

9. Sew one 2" x 10¹/₂" Fabric A piece, matching unit from step 6, unit from step 7, unit from step 8, and matching 2" x 10¹/₂" Fabric A piece in order shown. Press. Block measures 10¹/₂" x 16¹/₂".

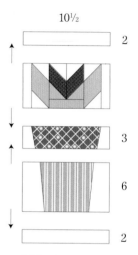

10¹/₂

2

3

6

2

Make 3
(1 of each variation)
Block measures 10¹/₂ x 16¹/₂

Turn this seam under for appliqué

Flowerpot Base Template
for Hand Appliqué
Cut one on fold for each block

Place on fold

Assembly

1. Referring to quilt photo on page 10 and quilt layout, position and sew blocks together. Press.

2. Measure quilt through center from side to side. Trim two 1½"-wide First Border strips to that measurement. Sew to top and bottom of quilt. Press seams toward borders.

3. Measure quilt through center from top to bottom including borders just added. Cut remaining 1½"-wide First Border strip into two strips to that measurement. Sew to sides of quilt. Press.

4. Sew 2"-wide Second Border strips end to end to make one continuous 2"-wide strip. Refer to Adding the Borders on page 80 to fit, trim, and sew 2"-wide Second Border strips to top, bottom, and sides of quilt. Press.

5. We chose a plaid as our border and cut each strip in order to match the plaid. We measured and cut for the top 4½"-wide Outside Border as in step 2. Then we cut the side borders to match the top, and last of all cut the bottom border. Arrange borders to match each other before sewing to quilt. Press.

Layering and Finishing

1. Arrange and baste backing, batting, and top together referring to Layering the Quilt on page 80. Hand or machine quilt as desired.

2. We used bias strips for our binding. Refer to Making Bias Strips on page 78. Start with a 21" square to cut bias strips. You will need approximately 150" of 2¾"-wide bias binding strips. (If you prefer to make straight cut binding instead of bias, cut and join four 2¾" x 42" strips.) Refer to Binding the Quilt on page 80 to bind quilt.

3. Sew a button in the center of each flower, if desired.

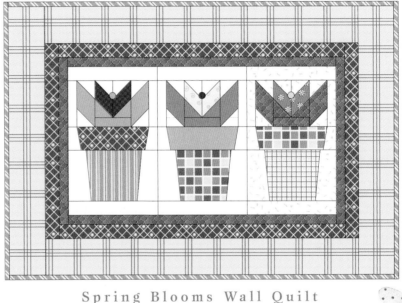

Spring Blooms Wall Quilt

Finished Size: 44" x 30"
Photo: page 10

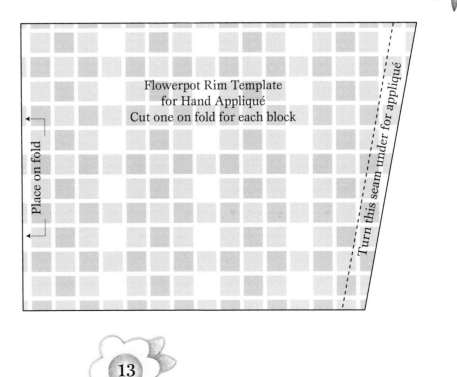

Flowerpot Rim Template
for Hand Appliqué
Cut one on fold for each block

Place on fold

Turn this seam under for appliqué

13

Terrific Tulips
Window Covering

A painted watering can sprinkles garden-sweet charm on a colorful curtain that's sure to bring a bright touch of spring! Tender tulips grow in a row on this sweet and easy curtain. Adapt this pattern to fit your window or use this idea to decorate a shower curtain, bed skirt, or valance. Our pieced tulips are so easy, you'll want to "grow" a roomful.

Fabric Requirements and Cutting Instructions

Read all instructions before beginning and use 1/4"-wide seam allowances throughout. Read Cutting the Strips and Pieces on page 78 prior to cutting fabrics. Fabric Requirements depend on the size of your window.

Terrific Tulips Window Covering	FIRST CUT	
	Number of Strips or Pieces	Dimensions
Fabric A Flower Background *for each flower*	6*	2 1/2" squares
Fabric B Leaves *for each flower*	2*	2 1/2" x 5 1/2"
	2*	2 1/2" squares
	1*	1 1/2" x 4 1/2"
Fabric C Flower *for each flower*	2*	2 1/2" x 4 1/2"
Fabric D Curtain **to be determined by size of window*	1	Curtain top**
	1	Curtain Bottom**
	2	2 1/2" x 5 1/2"
Assorted Buttons		

Determining Curtain Size

1. Measure the width of window. Multiply width measurement by 1 1/2 – 2 to determine finished curtain width. The measurement needs to be divisible by 8 since each finished flower block is 8" wide. This will determine the number of Flower Blocks needed for curtain. Add 5" to final measurement to determine fabric width.

2. Determine curtain rod placement and desired finished length of curtain.
Curtain Top Fabric - Determine the width needed for the rod pocket, multiply by two, then add 1 1/2". Add this measurement to desired finished curtain length. Decide how much fabric you want below the flower row (we used 2"), and subtract this amount and 5" (for the flower row) from your length measurement.
Curtain Bottom Fabric - Width is the same as determined in

step 1. The length will be two times the number of inches you want below the flower row, plus 5 3/4". Using measurements from steps 1 and 2, cut Curtain Top and Bottom pieces from Fabric D.

Flower Block Row

1. Refer to Spring Blooms Wall Quilt steps 1 through 5 to make desired number of Flower Blocks.

2. Sew flower units together side by side in one long row to make Flower Block Row. Press seams. Sew row between two 2 1/2" x 5 1/2" Fabric D pieces. Press.

Assembly

1. Sew Flower Block Row from step 2 between Curtain Top and Curtain Bottom fabrics. Press seams away from flower row.

2. Turn side edges of curtain under 1", press, and turn under again 1" to form side hems. Press. Stitch along first folded edge.

3. Turn top edge of curtain under 1/4" and press. To make rod pocket, fold top edge of curtain again by the width needed for the rod pocket plus 3/4". Stitch along First Rod Pocket Fold to form the bottom of rod pocket. Stitch again 1/2" away from top of curtain to make a decorative edge and to form pocket for the curtain rod.

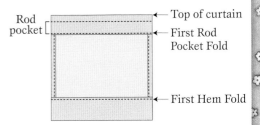

4. For border and hem, turn raw edge under 1/4" and press. Turn fabric again to enclose back of flower row in hem. We made our hem 7 1/4" deep to make a 2" border below the flowers and to cover the raw seams on the flower row. Pin hem in place and slipstitch to fasten or edge stitch along top edge of First Hem Fold. Press. Sew a button in the center of each flower, if desired. Insert rod through the rod pocket and hang curtain.

Watering Can Accent

A colorful watering can brings garden-fresh charm to the window treatment. A child-size tin watering can was painted in colors to match the curtain. To paint a tin or metal watering can, first wash can with vinegar, rinse well, and allow to dry. Spray watering can with a flat metal primer to prepare the surface for painting. Use acrylic paints to highlight different areas of the watering can. Be sure to allow each coat of paint to dry thoroughly before moving to the next color. Add polka dots by dipping the round wooden handle of a sponge paintbrush into yellow paint, then applying to the watering can. When complete and thoroughly dry, spray with a matte varnish. Use 1/4"-wide ribbon and cup hooks to suspend your watering can in the window. Tilt the watering can so that it looks like it is watering the tulip border.

Finished Size: 46" x 64½"

Chicks and Bunnies
Crib Quilt

Sweet as a lullaby, comfy as a cloud ... this spring-fresh, cuddly crib quilt transforms everyday naptime into a special event! Baby chicks and floppy-eared bunnies peek through tall grass and delicate posies, providing perfect company for little one's journey to dreamland.

Fabric Requirements and Cutting Instructions

Read all instructions before beginning and use 1/4"-wide seam allowances throughout. Read Cutting the Strips and Pieces on page 78 prior to cutting fabrics.

Chicks and Bunnies Crib Quilt 46" x 64 1/2"	FIRST CUT		SECOND CUT	
	Number of Strips or Pieces	Dimensions	Number of Pieces	Dimensions
Fabric A Background Row 1 *1/2 yard*	1	4 1/2" x 42"	1	4 1/2" x 13 1/2"
			3	4 1/2" x 2 1/2"
			3	4 1/2" x 1 1/2"
	2	2 1/2" x 42"	3	2 1/2" x 7 1/2"
			12	2 1/2" squares
			9	2 1/2" x 1 1/2"
	4	1 1/2" x 42"	3	1 1/2" x 7 1/2"
			6	1 1/2" x 6 1/2"
			5	1 1/2" x 5 1/2"
			23	1 1/2" squares
Fabric B Background Row 2 and Flower Background *1 yard**	1	13 1/2" x 42"	1	13 1/2" x 4 1/2"
			2	6 1/2" x 2 1/2"
			4	6 1/2" x 1 1/2"
			5	5 1/2" x 1 1/2"
			2	4 1/2" x 3 1/2"
			1	4 1/2" x 2 1/2"
			3	4 1/2" x 1 1/2"
			2	3 1/2" x 8 1/2"
	2	4 1/2" x 42"	2	4 1/2" x 36 1/2"
	2	2 1/2" x 42"	1	2 1/2" x 7 1/2"
			12	2 1/2" squares
			3	2 1/2" x 1 1/2"
	1	1 1/2" x 42"	1	1 1/2" x 7 1/2"
			21	1 1/2" squares
Fabric C Background Row 3 *5/8 yard**	1	13 1/2" x 42"	1	13 1/2" x 8 1/2"
			1	6 1/2" x 2 1/2"
			7	6 1/2" x 1 1/2"
			6	5 1/2" x 1 1/2"
			1	4 1/2" x 3 1/2"
			1	4 1/2" x 2 1/2"
			2	4 1/2" x 1 1/2"
			1	3 1/2" x 8 1/2"
	1	2 1/2" x 42"	1	2 1/2" x 7 1/2"
			8	2 1/2" squares
			3	2 1/2" x 1 1/2"
	1	1 1/2" x 42"	1	1 1/2" x 7 1/2"
			21	1 1/2" squares

We used directional fabric for Fabrics B and C. The cut listed first (strip width) runs parallel to selvage.

Because of the variety of pieces, we recommend labeling each piece with its measurements.

Chart continued on next page

Making the Chick Blocks

You'll be making a total of five Chick Blocks: three with Background Fabric A and one each with Background Fabric B and Fabric C.

Unfinished blocks measure 7 1/2" x 14 1/2". Whenever possible, use the Assembly Line Method on page 78. Press in the direction of arrows.

1. Refer to Quick Corner Triangles on page 78. Sew four 1 1/2" Fabric A squares to 4 1/2" Fabric D square as shown. Press. Make three units using Fabrics A and D, one unit using Fabrics B and D, and one unit using Fabrics C and D.

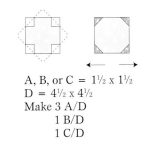

A, B, or C = 1 1/2 x 1 1/2
D = 4 1/2 x 4 1/2
Make 3 A/D
    1 B/D
    1 C/D

2. Making quick corner triangle units, sew one 1 1/2" Fabric F square to a 2 1/2" x 1 1/2" Fabric A piece as shown. Press. Make five, three using Fabrics A and F, one using Fabrics B and F, and one using Fabrics C and F.

F = 1 1/2 x 1 1/2
A, B, or C = 2 1/2 x 1 1/2
Make 3 A/F
    1 B/F
    1 C/F

Chicks and Bunnies Crib Quilt continued	FIRST CUT	
	Number of Strips or Pieces	Dimensions
Fabric D Chicks *1/4 yard each of five fabrics*	1*	6 1/2" square
	1*	4 1/2" square
	1*	1 1/2" square
Fabric E Bunnies *1/4 yard each of three fabrics*	1*	6 1/2" square
	1*	4 1/2" square
Fabric F Chick Beak *scrap*	5	1 1/2" squares
Fabric G Grass *1/4 yard*	4	1 1/2" x 8 1/2"
	5	1 1/2" x 7 1/2"
	2	1 1/2" x 4 1/2"
	1	1" x 36 1/2"
Fabric H Grass Blades, Stems, and Leaves *Assorted scraps to total 1 yard*	16	9 1/2" x 1 1/2"
	17	8 1/2" x 1 1/2"
	2	3 1/2" x 24"
	3	11" x 1"
	1	8" x 1"
Fabric I Patchwork Sashing and Bows *assorted scraps*	36	2 1/2" squares
	4	8 1/2" x 2"

Cut for each fabric
Flowers, Flower Centers, Chick Feet, Bunny Ears, Bunny Tails - Assorted scraps
Embroidery floss, perle cotton
Template plastic

BORDERS

First Border *1/3 yard*	5	1 1/2" x 42"
Outside Border *3/4 yard*	6	4" x 42"
Binding *5/8 yard*	6	2 3/4" x 42"

Backing - 3 yards
Batting - 53" x 72"

Tracing Line _____
Stitching Line _ _ _ _ _ _ _ _ _

tack to bunny

Bunny Ear Template
Cut 4 and 4 reversed

Leave open for turning

Eye

Leaf Template
Cut 4 and 4 reversed

Template for Yo-yo Bunny Tail
Cut 2

3. Sew one matching 2¹/₂" x 1¹/₂" Fabric A, B, or C piece to each unit from step 2 as shown. Press. Make three with Background A and one each with Backgrounds B and C.

1¹/₂

2¹/₂

Make 3 Background A
Make 1 each Background B and C

4. Sew each unit from step 1 between matching 4¹/₂" x 2¹/₂" Fabric A, B, or C piece and matching unit from step 3 as shown. Press. Make three with Background A and one each with Backgrounds B and C.

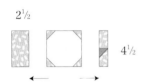

2¹/₂

4¹/₂

Make 3 Background A
Make 1 each Background B and C

5. Making quick corner triangle units, sew four matching 2¹/₂" Fabric A, B, or C squares to each 6¹/₂" Fabric D square as shown. Press. Make three units using Fabrics A and D, one unit using Fabrics B and D, and one unit using Fabrics C and D.

A, B, or C = 2¹/₂ x 2¹/₂
D = 6¹/₂ x 6¹/₂
Make 3 A/D
    1 B/D
    1 C/D

6. Making a quick corner triangle unit, sew one 1¹/₂" Fabric D square to a 4¹/₂" x 1¹/₂" Fabric A, B, or C piece as shown. Press. Make three units using Fabrics A and D, one unit using Fabrics B and D, and one unit using Fabrics C and D.

D = 1¹/₂ x 1¹/₂
A, B, or C = 4¹/₂ x 1¹/₂
Make 3 A/D
    1 B/D
    1 C/D

7. Sew each unit from step 6 to a matching 2¹/₂" x 1¹/₂" Fabric A, B, or C piece as shown. Press. Make three with Background A and one each with Backgrounds B and C.

2¹/₂

1¹/₂

Make 3 Background A
Make 1 each Background B and C

8. Sew units from step 5 and step 7 in matching pairs as shown. Press. Make three with Background A and one each with Backgrounds B and C.

Make 3 Background A
Make 1 each Background B and C

9. Sew a 2¹/₂" x 7¹/₂" Fabric A piece, matching units from step 4 and step 8, 1¹/₂" x 7¹/₂" Fabric A piece, and 1¹/₂" x 7¹/₂" Fabric G piece in order shown. Press. Make three to complete Fabric A Chick Block. Make one more of each Chick Block matching Background Fabrics B and C in each block. Block measures 7¹/₂" x 14¹/₂".

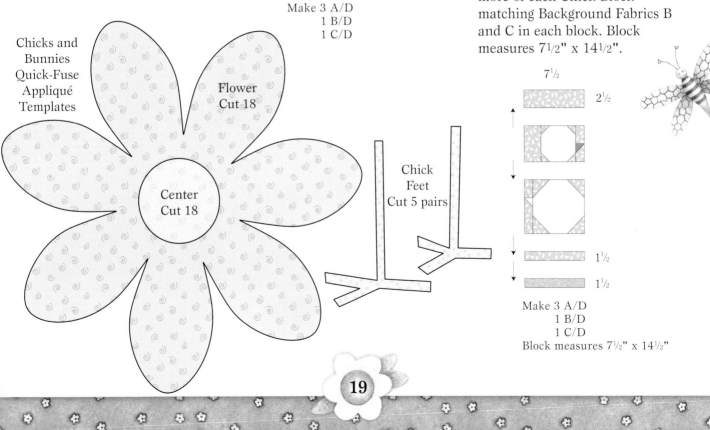

Chicks and Bunnies Quick-Fuse Appliqué Templates

Flower
Cut 18

Center
Cut 18

Chick Feet
Cut 5 pairs

7¹/₂

2¹/₂

1¹/₂

1¹/₂

Make 3 A/D
    1 B/D
    1 C/D
Block measures 7¹/₂" x 14¹/₂"

Making the Bunny Blocks

You'll be making a total of three Bunny Blocks: two with Fabric B and one with Fabric C. Unfinished blocks measure 8½" x 14½". Whenever possible, use the Assembly Line Method on page 78. Press in the direction of arrows.

1. Referring to Quick Corner Triangles on page 78, sew four matching 1½" Fabric B or C squares to each 4½" Fabric E square as shown. Press. Make two units using Fabrics B and E and one unit using Fabrics C and E.

B or C = 1½ x 1½
E = 4½ x 4½
Make 2 B/E
  1 C/E

2. Sew each unit from step 1 between matching 4½" x 1½" Fabric B or C Background piece and matching 4½" x 3½" Fabric B or C piece as shown. Press. Make two with Background B and one with Background C.

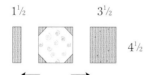

1½   3½

4½

Make 2 Background B
Make 1 Background C

3. Making quick corner triangle units, sew four matching 2½" Fabric B or C Background squares to each 6½" Fabric E square as shown. Press. Make two units using Fabrics B and E and one unit using Fabric C and E.

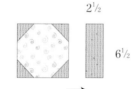

B or C = 2½ x 2½
E = 6½ x 6½
Make 2 B/E
  1 C/E

4. Sew one matching 6½" x 2½" Fabric B or C Background piece to each unit from step 3 as shown. Press. Make two units using Fabrics B and E and one unit using Fabric C and E.

2½

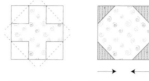

6½

Make 2 Background B
Make 1 Background C

5. Sew a 3½" x 8½" Fabric B or C Background piece, matching units from step 2 and step 4, and a 1½" x 8½" Fabric G piece in order shown. Press. Make two blocks using Fabric B and one block using Fabric C. Block measures 8½" x 14½".

8½

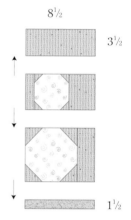

3½

1½

Make 2 Background B
Make 1 Background C
Block measures 8½" x 14½"

Grass Blade Units

1. Making quick corner triangle units, sew a 1½" Fabric A, B, or C square to each 8½" x 1½" Fabric H piece as shown. Press. Make six with Fabrics A and H, four with Fabrics B and H, and seven with Fabrics C and H.

A, B or C = 1½ x 1½
H = 8½ x 1½
Make 6 A/H
4 B/H
7 C/H

2. Sew a matching 1½" x 6½" Fabric A, B, or C piece to each unit from step 1 as shown. Press. Make seventeen.

6½

1½

Make 17

3. Making quick corner triangles, sew a 1½" Fabric A, B, or C square to each 9½" x 1½" Fabric H piece as shown. Press. Make five with Fabrics A and H, five with Fabrics B and H, and six with Fabrics C and H.

A, B, or C = 1½ x 1½
H = 9½ x 1½
Make 5 A/H
5 B/H
6 C/H

4. Sew a unit from step 3 to a matching 1½" x 5½" Fabric A, B, or C piece as shown. Press. Make sixteen.

5½

1½

Make 16

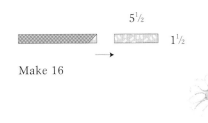

Dancing Daisies Pillow

Delightful daisies dance in the wind on this cute-as-a-button pillow. Retro fabrics and a flange border make this pillow as sweet as a spring breeze!

Finished Size: 18½" square

Fabric Requirements

Background (⅜ yard)
  12½" square
First Border (⅛ yard)
  two 1" x 13½" pieces
  two 1" x 12½" pieces
Second Border (¼ yard)
  two 3" x 18½" strips
  two 3" x 13½" pieces
Outside Border (⅛ yard)
  two ¾" x 19" strips
  two ¾" x 18½" strips
Stems and Leaves (⅛ yard)
Flowers (assorted scraps)
Lining and Batting - 21" square
Backing (⅜ yard)
  two 12" x 19" pieces
Lightweight fusible web (¼ yard)
Three 1" buttons
Pillow Form - 13"

Making the Pillow

1. *Refer to Quick-Fuse Appliqué on page 79 and appliqué templates on pages 18-19. Trace three flowers and leaves on paper side of fusible web. You may wish to reverse one of the leaves. For the stems, cut a 2" x 11" piece of fusible web and press it to the wrong side of a bias-cut piece of fabric. Cut fused piece into one ½" x 10½", one ½" x 9", and one ½" x 6½" pieces.*

2. *Refer to pillow photo to arrange and fuse stems, leaves, and flowers to 12½" Background square. Finish with machine satin stitch or decorative stitching as desired.*

3. *Sew two 1" x 12½" First Border pieces to top and bottom of pillow. Press toward borders. Sew remaining First Border pieces to sides. Press.*

4. *Repeat step 3 to add 3"-wide Second Borders and ¾"-wide Outside Borders to top, bottom, and sides. Press borders toward the center of Second Border.*

5. *Refer to Finishing Pillows on page 80 to quilt top and sew pillow backing to pillow. Press.*

6. *Referring to pillow photo, topstitch 2¾" from finished edge all around perimeter of pillow between First and Second Borders to form a flange.*

7. *Insert 13" form into pillow cover. To make your own pillow form, refer to Finishing Pillows on page 80.*

Assembly

1. Sew 4¹⁄₂" x 13¹⁄₂" Fabric A piece to 1¹⁄₂" x 4¹⁄₂" Fabric G piece as shown. Repeat using 13¹⁄₂" x 4¹⁄₂" Fabric B piece and 1¹⁄₂" x 4¹⁄₂" Fabric G piece. Press.

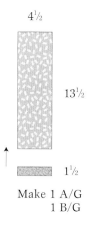

4¹⁄₂

13¹⁄₂

1¹⁄₂

Make 1 A/G
1 B/G

2. Sew 13¹⁄₂" x 8¹⁄₂" Fabric C piece to 1¹⁄₂" x 8¹⁄₂" Fabric G piece. Press.

8¹⁄₂

13¹⁄₂

1¹⁄₂

3. Arrange A/G unit from step 1, the three Chick Blocks, and all Grass Blade Units made with Fabric A to make a horizontal row as shown. Sew blocks and units together. Press and label Row 1.

Row 1   4¹⁄₂

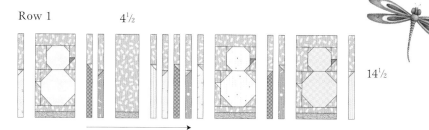

14¹⁄₂

4. Arrange B/G unit from step 1, two Bunny Blocks, one Chick Block, and all Grass Blade Units made with Fabric B to make a horizontal row as shown. Sew blocks and units together. Press and label Row 2.

Row 2   4¹⁄₂

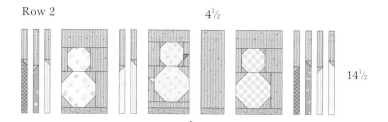

14¹⁄₂

5. Arrange unit from step 2, one Chick Block, one Bunny Block, and all Grass Blade Units made with Fabric C to make a horizontal row as shown. Sew blocks and units together. Press and label Row 3.

Row 3   8¹⁄₂

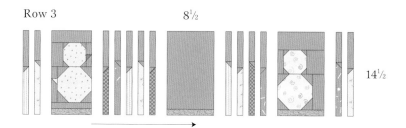

14¹⁄₂

6. Refer to quilt layout on page 23 and color photo on page 16. Arrange eighteen 2¹⁄₂" Fabric I squares in random order to make Patchwork Sashing row. Sew squares together. Press seams to one side. Make two rows.

7. Refer to quilt layout on page 23 and color photo on page 16. Arrange 4¹⁄₂" x 36¹⁄₂" Fabric B strip, 1" x 36¹⁄₂" Fabric G strip, Row 1, Patchwork Sashing from step 6, Row 2, Patchwork Sashing, Row 3, and 4¹⁄₂" x 36¹⁄₂" Fabric B strip. Sew rows and strips together. Press seams in one direction.

Appliqués

We used both quick-fuse and hand appliqué methods. We recommend making all templates with template plastic. If you prefer traditional hand appliqué, be sure to reverse all appliqué templates, and add 1/4" seam allowances when cutting appliqué pieces. Refer to Hand Appliqué directions on page 79 for additional guidance as needed.

1. Refer to Quick Fuse Appliqué on page 79. Trace appliqué templates on page 19 for flowers and flower centers. Use assorted scraps for the flowers and flower centers, and Fabric H scraps for stems.

2. Refer to quilt layout below and color photo on page 16 to position Fabric H stems on Backgrounds in Rows 1, 2, and 3.

3. Use one 11" x 1" stem each for Row 1 and Row 2, and one 8" x 1" and one 11" x 1" stem for Row 3. Turn under 1/4" on all edges and hand or machine appliqué in place.

4. Refer to quilt layout to position flowers and flower centers on stems. Position fourteen flowers and flower centers in Fabric B strips as shown. Fuse appliqués in place. Machine stitch around edges of appliqués with satin or decorative stitching as desired.

5. Trace Chick Feet template from page 19. Use fusible web and scraps to make five pairs of feet. Refer to quilt layout to position feet. Fuse appliqués in place. Machine stitch around edges of appliqués with satin or decorative stitching as desired.

6. If you plan to use the quilt in a baby's crib, use three strands of embroidery floss and a satin stitch to stitch eyes for chicks and bunnies. Since our quilt is for a wallhanging we added 3/8" buttons for the chicks' and bunnies' eyes after the quilt was quilted.

Borders

1. Sew 1 1/2"-wide First Border strips end to end to make one continuous 1 1/2"-wide strip. Press. Measure quilt through center from side to side. Trim two 1 1/2"-wide First Border strips to that measurement. Sew to top and bottom. Press seams toward border.

2. Measure quilt through center from top to bottom, including borders just added. Trim two 1 1/2"-wide First Border strips to that measurement. Sew to sides. Press.

3. Repeat steps 1 and 2 to join, fit, trim, and sew 4"-wide Outside Border strips to top, bottom, and sides of quilt. Press seams toward border.

Chicks and Bunnies Crib Quilt

Finished Size: 46" x 64 1/2"
Photo: page 16

23

Layering and Finishing

1. Cut backing crosswise into two equal pieces. Sew pieces together to make one 54" x 84" (approximate) backing piece. Arrange and baste backing, batting, and top together referring to Layering the Quilt directions on page 80.

2. Hand or machine quilt as desired.

3. Sew 2³/4"-wide binding strips end to end to make one continuous 2³/4"-wide binding strip. Refer to Binding the Quilt directions on page 80 and bind quilt.

4. For bunny ears, trace pattern on page 18 to make a template. Use scraps to trace and cut four regular and four reverse bunny ear pieces. Place regular and reverse bunny ear pieces right sides together in pairs. Using 1/4" seam, sew around edges, leaving an opening for turning. Trim corners, turn right side out, press, and hand stitch opening closed. Refer to quilt layout on page 23 and color photo on page 16 to position and appliqué or tack ears in place on each Bunny Block.

5. For leaves, fold two 3¹/2" x 24" Fabric H strips in half crosswise, right sides together. Trace four leaves and four reversed on each Fabric H piece. Stitch on traced line. Cut out leaf shape ³/16" away from stitched line. Clip corners. Cut a slit in one side of leaf shape and turn right side out. Press and hand stitch opening closed. Refer to quilt photo on page 16 and quilt layout on page 23 to position leaves on quilt. Stitch through the lengthwise center of leaves and all layers of quilt, by hand or machine, to attach leaves.

6. For each bow, fold one 8¹/2" x 2" Fabric I piece in half crosswise. Stitch raw edges together with 1/4"-wide seams, leaving an opening for turning. Clip corners, turn, press, and hand stitch opening closed. Tie a knot in center of fabric and stitch to chick at neck or on head.

7. For bunny whiskers, thread a needle with a 48" strand of perle cotton doubled. Take a 1/8" stitch, pulling thread through layers of quilt until there is a 4" tail. Cut thread leaving a 4" tail on both sides. Take another stitch perpendicular to first stitch leaving 4" tails. Tie threads securely and trim as desired.

Making Yo-yos

1. For yo-yo bunny tails, trace pattern on page 18 to make a template, and use scraps to make two yo-yos.

2. Trace yo-yo template on wrong side of fabric and cut out on drawn line.

3. Hold the circle with the wrong side facing you. Fold edge toward you turning 1/4" and use quilting thread to sew short running stitches close to folded edge.

Wrong side

4. Pull thread tightly to gather into a smaller circle. Make several invisible "tacking" stitches to secure the thread.

5. Refer to color photo on page 16 and quilt layout on page 23 to position and tack yo-yo bunny tails in place on two bunny blocks.

Signs of Spring Wall Quilt

A sweet little chick and adorable bunny rejoice in the coming of spring on this whimsical wallhanging. Make it to match the Chicks and Bunnies Crib Quilt for a special baby, or display it in your home to give spring a winsome welcome!

Finished Size: 41" x 27 1/2"

Fabric Requirements

Fabric B Flower Background
(1/3 yard) - two 4 1/2" x 36 1/2" strips
Fabric C Background (5/8 yard)
  refer to Cutting Chart on page 17
Fabric D Chick (1/4 yard)
  one 6 1/2" square
  one 4 1/2" square
  one 1 1/2" square
Fabric E Bunny (1/4 yard)
  one 6 1/2" square
  one 4 1/2" square
Fabric F Chick Beak (Scrap)
  one 1 1/2" square
Fabric G Grass (1/8 yard)
  two 1 1/2" x 8 1/2" pieces
  one 1 1/2" x 7 1/2" piece
  one 1" x 36 1/2" strip
Fabric H Grass Blades, Stems, and Leaves (Assorted scraps)
  seven 1 1/2" x 8 1/2" pieces
  six 1 1/2" x 9 1/2" pieces
  one 1" x 11" piece
  one 1" x 8" piece
Flower, Flower Centers, Bows, Bunny Ear, Bunny Tail (Assorted scraps)
Accent Border (1/6 yard)
  four 1" x 42" strips
Outside Border (1/3 yard)
  four 2" x 42" strips
Binding (3/8 yard)
  four 2 3/4" x 42" strips
Backing (7/8 yard)
  fabric must be 45" wide
Batting - 45" x 31 1/2" piece
Perle cotton

Making the Wall Quilt

1. Refer to Chicks and Bunnies Crib Quilt, pages 17-20 to make one Chick Block and one Bunny Block.

2. Follow all steps in Grass Blade Units on page 21 to make seven units in steps 1 and 2 and six units in steps 3 and 4, using Fabrics C and H.

3. Follow Assembly steps 2 and 5 on page 22 to assemble chick and bunny Row 3.

4. Referring to quilt layout above, arrange 4 1/2" x 36 1/2" Fabric B strip, 1" x 36 1/2" Fabric G strip, chick and bunny row, and 4 1/2" x 36 1/2" Fabric B strip. Sew strips and row together. Press seams in one direction.

5. Refer to Adding the Borders on page 80 to add 1"-wide First and 2"-wide Outside Border strips to top, bottom, and sides of quilt.

6. Refer to Appliqués on page 23 in Chicks and Bunnies Crib Quilt to add two stems and sixteen Flower and Flower Center appliqués to wall quilt.

7. Refer to Layering the Quilt and Binding the Quilt on page 80 to baste, quilt, and bind quilt.

8. Refer to Layering and Finishing the Quilt on page 24, steps 4-6 to add four leaves, one bow, and one bunny ear. Refer to Making Yo-yos at left for bunny tail.

Finished Size: 39½" x 48"

By the Sea
Wall Quilt

You can almost feel the sea breeze and hear the ocean waves with this sensational seashore scene. Prairie point waves beat against the rocks, while the illusion of shimmering water is created with softly colored fabric strips. Paper-piecing for the lighthouse and sailboat and the quick corner triangle construction of the rocky shore make this project as easy-going as a summer day!

Fabric Requirements and Cutting Instructions

Read all instructions before beginning and use ¼"-wide seam allowances throughout. Read Cutting the Strips and Pieces on page 78 prior to cutting fabrics.

By the Sea Wall Quilt 39½" x 48"	FIRST CUT Number of Strips or Pieces	Dimensions
Fabric A Sky ½ yard ⅜ yard for non-directional fabric	1	6" x 7½"
	1	5½" x 29½"
	1	5½" x 4½"
	1	5" x 21½"
	1	3½" x 10½"
Fabric B Whitecaps Assorted fabrics to total ¼ yard	3	3" squares
	15	2½" squares
	17	2" squares
	2	1½" squares
Fabric C Light Water ¼ yard	1	2½" x 21½"
	1	2½" x 5½"
	1	2½" x 3½"
	2	2½" squares
	1	1½" x 7½"
	1	1½" x 4½"
	1	1½" x 3½"
	1	1½" square
Fabric D Light/Medium Water ⅔ yard ¼ yard for non-directional fabric	1	2½" x 17½"
	1	2½" square
	1	2" x 16½"
	1	2" x 9½"
	1	2" x 7½"
	1	2" square
	1	1½" x 21½"
	1	1½" x 3½"
	1	1½" square
Fabric E Medium Water ⅓ yard	1	2½" square
	2	2" x 21½"
	1	2" x 3½"
	1	1½" x 21½"
	1	1½" x 10½"
	1	1½" x 8½"
	1	1½" x 7½"
	1	1½" x 6½"
	1	1½" x 3½"
	9	1½" squares
Fabric F Dark Water ¼ yard	1	2½" x 9½"
	2	2½" squares
	1	2" x 21½"
	1	2" x 3½"
	1	1½" x 9½"
	1	1½" x 7½"
	1	1" x 4½"

By the Sea Wall Quilt continued	FIRST CUT Number of Strips or Pieces	Dimensions
Fabric G Light Rocks ⅓ yard	1	8½" x 6"
	1	2½" x 12½"
	2	2½" x 4"
	1	2" square
Fabric H Light/Medium Rocks ¼ yard	1	4" x 10½"
	1	2½" x 7½"
	1	2½" x 4½"
	1	2½" square
	1	1½" x 2½"
	1	1½" x 2"
	1	1½" square
Fabric I Medium Rocks ⅙ yard	1	3½" x 7½"
	1	3½" x 2½"
	1	3" square
	1	2½" x 5½"
	1	2½" square
	1	1½" x 4"
	2	1½" squares
Fabric J Dark Rocks ⅙ yard	1	5" x 7½"
	1	2½" x 5½"
	1	2" x 3½"
	1	1½" x 3½"

BORDERS		
First Border 1⅓ yards **OR** ⅓ yard for non-directional fabric	4	1¾" x 47½"
	5	1¾" x 42"
Second Border ⅙ yard	4	1" x 42"
Outside Border ½ yard	4	3½" x 42"
Binding ½ yard	5	2¾" x 42"

Paper-pieced blocks - Assorted scraps
Backing - 1½ yards (Must be 44" or wider)
Batting - 44" x 52"

Making the Blocks

You will be using a combination of techniques for this quilt, including paper-foundation piecing, quick corner triangles, and prairie points.

Foundation-Pieced Blocks

Copy paper-piecing Sections A, B, C, D, and E for the Lighthouse Block (on pages 32, 34-35), and Sections A, B, and C for the Sailboat Block (on pages 36-37). *If using a copier, be sure to compare the copy to the original to make sure your pattern is accurate.*
Cut paper-piecing copies larger than trim line on all sides. Blocks will be cut on **trim line** after they are completed.

Lighthouse Block

1. Beginning with Lighthouse Section D, place lighthouse fabric right side up over shape 1 on blank (unprinted) side of Section D paper-piecing pattern, centering it over area labeled "1". Pin to paper using flat flower-head pins. Be sure to cover entire area extending at least 1/2" on all sides of shape 1. If it is difficult to see through paper, hold layers up to light.

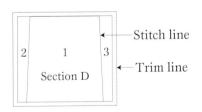

Section D
Stitch line
Trim line

2. Turn paper to printed side. Fold paper along stitch line between 1 and 2. Trim fabric 1/4" from stitch line. Unfold paper.

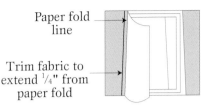

Paper fold line

Trim fabric to extend 1/4" from paper fold

3. With right sides together, position one water fabric scrap on lighthouse fabric, matching edges with the piece just trimmed. Hold layers up to light to see through to pattern line. Be sure all fabrics extend beyond trim line of pattern by at least 1/4".

4. With paper printed side up, sew through paper and both layers of fabric. Stitch on line using a very short stitch (14 to 16 stitches per inch). Be sure to begin and end stitching 1/4" beyond line.

5. Flip Section 2 (water) fabric piece over to cover up seam line. Press.

6. Repeat steps 2 through 5 to sew Section 3 (water) piece.

7. Turn unit paper-side up, stay-stitch just inside trim line. Trim fabric along paper pattern trim line.

8. Repeat steps 1 through 7 to complete Lighthouse Sections A, B, C, and E, adding pieces in numerical order. Referring to quilt layout on page 33, sew units together. Press seams open. Carefully remove paper from back of block. Block measures 5 1/2" x 18 1/2".

Sailboat Block

1. Following steps 1 through 7 for Lighthouse Block, sew Sections A, B, and C for sailboat.

2. Sew Sections A and B together. Press seam open. Sew Section C to unit A/B. Block measures 10 1/2" x 7". Press seams open.

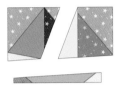

Whitecaps (Prairie Points)

1. Fold one 3" Fabric B square in half diagonally, with wrong sides together. Press. Fold again as shown. Make three. Raw edges will be together; align them with the raw edges of the strips when you position them later.

Fold   Fold again

Fold Fold

Make 3 large
15 med/large
17 medium
2 small

2. Repeat step 1 to make fifteen 2 1/2" (medium-large) squares, seventeen 2" (medium) squares, and two 1 1/2" (small) squares.

Assembling the Center Panel

1. Sew one 1½" x 4½" Fabric C piece between 5½" x 4½" Fabric A and 1" x 4½" Fabric F pieces. Sew 6" x 7½" Fabric A piece to 1½" x 7½" Fabric C piece. Press.

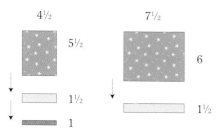

2. Sew Sailboat Block between units from step 1 as shown. Press.

3. Sew one 5" x 21½" Fabric A strip to the top of unit from step 2.

4. Referring to quilt layout on page 33, position five Whitecaps, matching raw edges along the bottom of unit from step 3, and pin in place.

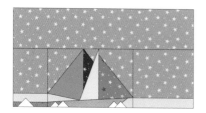

5. Sew one 1½" x 21½" Fabric E strip to unit from step 4. Press. Position Whitecap on unit prior to sewing next strip. Sew one 1½" x 21½" Fabric D strip to unit. Press. Repeat process to position Whitecaps and sew one 2" x 21½" Fabric E strip, one 2" x 21½" Fabric F strip, and one 2½" x 21½" Fabric C strip as shown. Press.

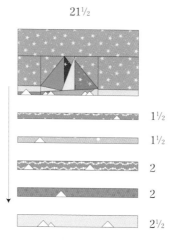

Note: Follow this procedure throughout entire project, positioning Whitecaps along the bottom edge of unit prior to sewing on next piece.

6. Sew 3½" x 10½" Fabric A piece, one 1½" x 3½" Fabric C piece, one 1½" x 3½" Fabric E piece, one 1½" x 3½" Fabric D piece (with Whitecap), one 2" x 3½" Fabric E piece, one 2" x 3½" Fabric F piece (with Whitecap), and one 2½" x 3½" Fabric C piece as shown. Press.

Tabletop Seascape

Escape to the seaside every time you light a candle with this easy-to-make tabletop accessory.

Materials Needed
Terra cotta flowerpot saucer
Gesso
Acrylic paints in light, medium, and dark blue
Sea sponge
Assorted paintbrushes
Matte spray varnish
Candle
Sand
Seashells

Paint inside and outside of clean, dry, terra cotta saucer with gesso to prepare it for painting. When dry, apply a basecoat of dark blue paint to the saucer. Allow to dry.

Dampen sea sponge, wring thoroughly, then dip in medium blue paint and blot on a paper towel. Sponge medium blue over dark blue basecoat. Work sponge lightly with a tapping motion over the basecoat until medium blue sponging is well blended.

Use the same process and a very light touch to add some light blue highlights to the rim of the saucer. When dry, spray saucer with matte spray varnish.

Fill saucer with sand and place candle in the middle. Arrange seashells, coral, and rocks around the candle. If desired, place a glass hurricane globe around the candle before arranging shells.

7. Sew Lighthouse Block between unit from step 5 and unit from step 6 as shown. Press. Sew 5½" x 29½" Fabric A piece to top. Press.

29½

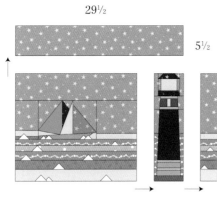

5½

8. Referring to Quick Corner Triangles on page 78, sew 1½" Fabric E square to 1½" x 3½" Fabric J piece as shown. Sew this unit to a 1½" x 6½" Fabric E piece. Press.

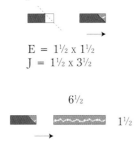

E = 1½ x 1½
J = 1½ x 3½

6½

1½

9. Making a quick corner triangle unit, sew 1½" Fabric I square to 1½" x 9½" Fabric F piece as shown. Press.

I = 1½ x 1½
F = 1½ x 9½

10. Add one Whitecap to unit from step 8, as shown. Then sew this unit to unit from step 9. Press.

11. Making quick corner triangle units, sew two 1½" Fabric E squares to 3½" x 2½" Fabric I piece as shown. Press. Sew this unit to unit from step 10 as shown. Press.

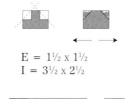

E = 1½ x 1½
I = 3½ x 2½

12. Position Whitecap on 1½" x 7½" Fabric E piece, then sew unit to a 1½" x 7½" Fabric F piece. Press. Sew this unit to unit from step 11. Position Whitecap to lower piece as shown.

7½

1½

1½

13. Making a quick corner triangle unit, sew 2" Fabric D square to 2" x 3½" Fabric J piece as shown. Press. Sew this unit to 2" x 16½" Fabric D piece. Press.

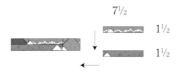

D = 2 x 2
J = 2 x 3½

16½

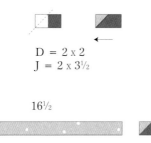

2

14. Sew unit from step 13 to the bottom of unit from step 12. Press. Position Whitecap on lower piece as shown.

15. Making a quick corner triangle unit, sew 1½" Fabric E square to 2½" x 4" Fabric G piece. Press. Sew this unit to unit in step 14 as shown. Press.

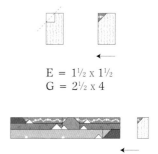

E = 1½ x 1½
G = 2½ x 4

16. Making quick corner triangle units, sew two 1½" Fabric E squares to 2½" x 7½" Fabric H piece as shown. Sew one 1½" Fabric E square to a 2½" x 4½" Fabric H piece. Press.

E = 1½ x 1½
H = 2½ x 7½

E = 1½ x 1½
H = 2½ x 4½

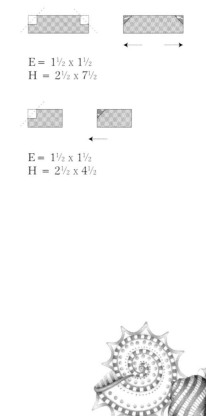

17. Making a quick corner triangle unit, sew 1½" Fabric E square to 1½" x 2½" Fabric H piece as shown. Press. Sew this unit to 1½" x 8½" Fabric E piece. Press.

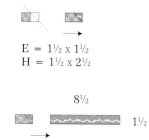

E = 1½ x 1½
H = 1½ x 2½

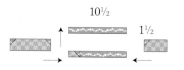

18. Sew unit from step 17 to 1½" x 10½" Fabric E piece. Press. Sew this unit between units from step 16 as shown. Press.

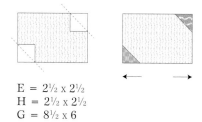

19. Making quick corner triangle units, sew 2½" Fabric H square and 2½" Fabric E square to 8½" x 6" Fabric G piece as shown. Press.

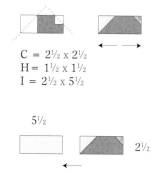

E = 2½ x 2½
H = 2½ x 2½
G = 8½ x 6

20. Sew unit from step 15 to unit from step 18. Press. Sew this unit to unit from step 19 as shown. Press. Position and pin four Whitecaps on unit.

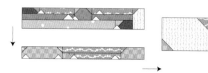

21. Sew unit from step 20 to unit from step 7. Press.

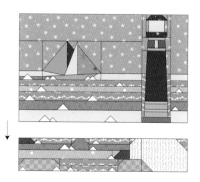

22. Making quick corner triangle units, sew one 1½" and one 2½" Fabric C square to a 3½" x 7½" Fabric I piece as shown. Press.

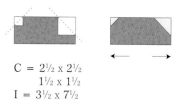

C = 2½ x 2½
    1½ x 1½
I = 3½ x 7½

23. Making quick corner triangle units, sew one 2½" and one 3" Fabric I square to 5" x 7½" Fabric J piece as shown. Press.

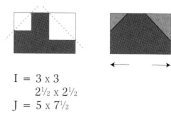

I = 3 x 3
    2½ x 2½
J = 5 x 7½

24. Sew unit from step 22 between 2" x 7½" Fabric D piece and unit from step 23 as shown. Press.

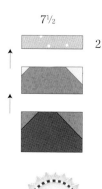

25. Making a quick corner triangle unit, sew 1½" Fabric D square to 1½" x 2" Fabric H piece. Press. Sew to 2" x 9½" Fabric D piece as shown. Press.

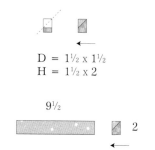

D = 1½ x 1½
H = 1½ x 2

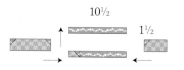

26. Making quick corner triangle units, sew 2½" Fabric C square and 1½" Fabric H square to a 2½" x 5½" Fabric I piece as shown. Press. Sew this unit to 2½" x 5½" Fabric C piece. Press.

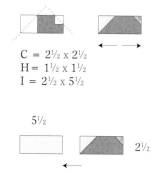

C = 2½ x 2½
H = 1½ x 1½
I = 2½ x 5½

27. Position a Whitecap on lower edge of unit from step 25. Sew unit to unit from step 26 as shown. Press.

28. Making a quick corner triangle unit, sew 2" Fabric G square to 4" x 10½" Fabric H piece as shown. Press. Sew this unit to 2½" x 4" Fabric G piece. Press.

G = 2 x 2
H = 4 x 10½

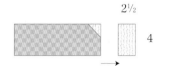

29. Sew unit from step 28 to unit from step 27. Press.

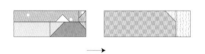

30. Making a quick corner triangle unit, sew 1½" Fabric E square to a 1½" x 4" Fabric I piece. Press.

E = 1½ x 1½
I = 1½ x 4

31. Making a quick corner triangle unit, sew 1½" Fabric I square to 2½" x 9½" Fabric F piece. Press. Sew two 2½" Fabric F squares to 2½" x 12½" Fabric G piece as shown. Press.

I = 1½ x 1½
F = 2½ x 9½

F = 2½ x 2½
G = 2½ x 12½

32. Sew units from step 31 together as shown. Position one Whitecap on 2" x 21½" Fabric E piece then sew to unit. Press. Sew this unit to unit from step 30 as shown. Press.

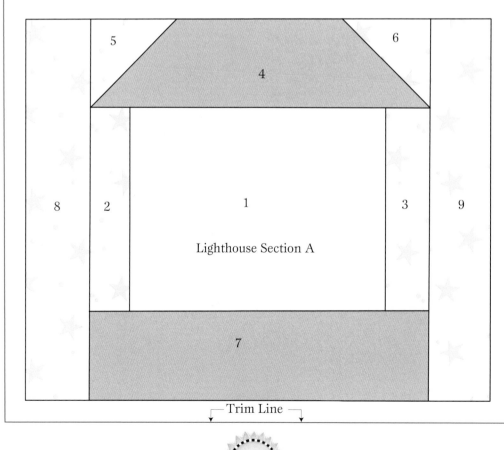

Lighthouse Section A

Trim Line

33. Making a quick corner triangle unit, sew 2¹⁄₂" Fabric D square to 2¹⁄₂" x 5¹⁄₂" Fabric J piece. Press. Sew this unit to 2¹⁄₂" x 17¹⁄₂" Fabric D piece as shown. Press.

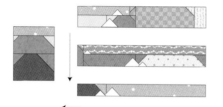

D = 2¹⁄₂ x 2¹⁄₂
J = 2¹⁄₂ x 5¹⁄₂

34. Position one Whitecap on unit from step 29, and two Whitecaps on unit from step 32. Sew units together. Press. Sew this unit to unit from step 33, and then sew to unit from step 24. Press. Position two Whitecaps on lower edge. Referring to layout, sew unit to unit from step 21. Press. Quilt top measures 29¹⁄₂" x 38" before borders are added.

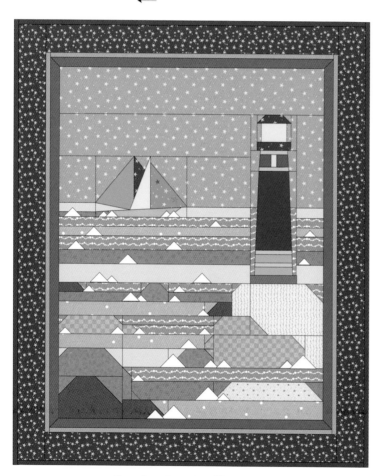

By the Sea Wall Quilt

Finished Size: 39¹⁄2" x 48"
Photo: page 26

Add More Seaside Decor to Your Home

Remember walking barefoot in the sand ... listening to the ocean's roar ...

When you use your seashell souvenirs to decorate your home you'll think of seaside adventures every time you look around! Show off your tidewater treasures with these easy decorating ideas:

Fill decorative containers of varying heights with seashells and place on your mantel. Group with some distinctive pieces of driftwood and water polished rocks to make a mantelpiece seascape.

Add some shells to a tabletop fountain or a backyard birdbath.

Place shells, rocks, and clear marbles in the bottom of a fish bowl or a clear salad bowl and fill with water. Place floating fish candles in the water and light for an instant centerpiece.

Paint a terra cotta flowerpot ivory, then cover with shells using tile adhesive. Fill in gaps with tile grout. Spray with sealer for outdoor use.

Borders

1. Refer to Mitered Borders on page 80. For directional fabric, sew 1¾" x 47½" strips to top, bottom, and sides of quilt, mitering corners.

2. For non-directional fabric, sew 1¾"-wide First Border strips end to end to make one continuous 1¾"-wide strip. Refer to Adding the Borders on page 80 to fit, trim, and sew 1¾"-wide First Border strip to top, bottom, and sides of quilt.

3. Repeat step 2 to join, fit, trim and sew 1"-wide Second Border strips and 3½"-wide Outside Border strips to top, bottom, and sides of quilt.

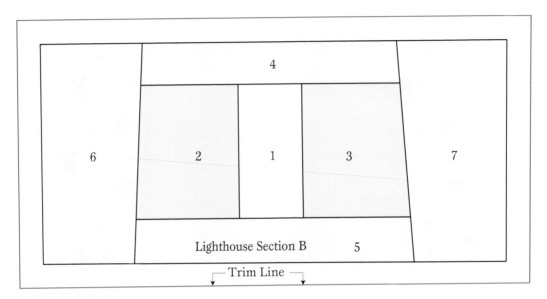

Lighthouse Section B

Trim Line

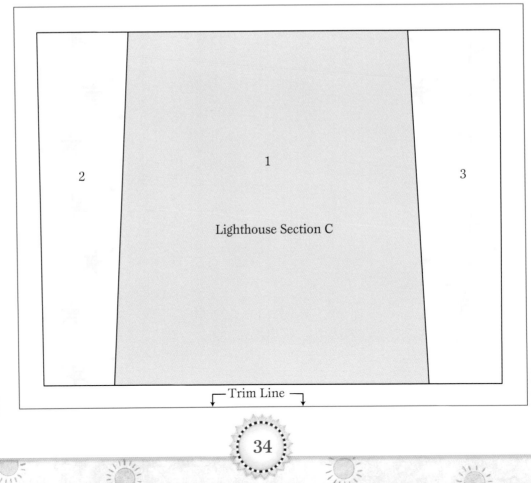

Lighthouse Section C

Trim Line

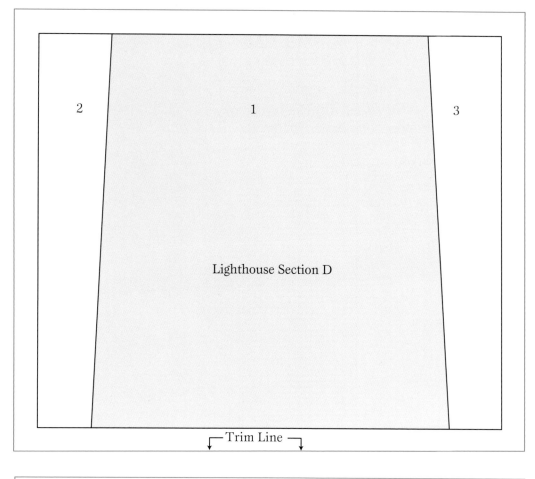

2   1   3

Lighthouse Section D

┌─ Trim Line ┐

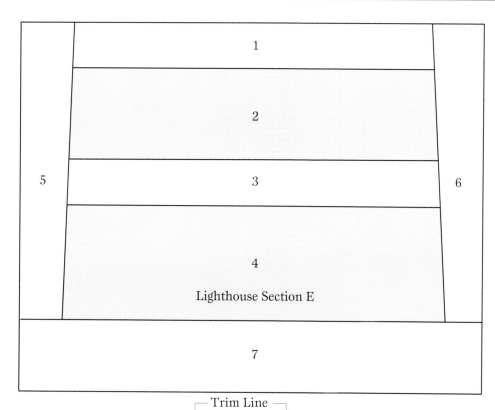

1

2

5   3   6

4

Lighthouse Section E

7

┌─ Trim Line ┐

Layering and Finishing

1. Arrange and baste backing, batting, and top together referring to Layering the Quilt on page 80.

2. Hand or machine quilt as desired.

3. Sew 2¾"-wide Binding strips end to end to make one continuous 2¾"-wide strip. Refer to Binding the Quilt directions on page 80 and bind quilt to finish.

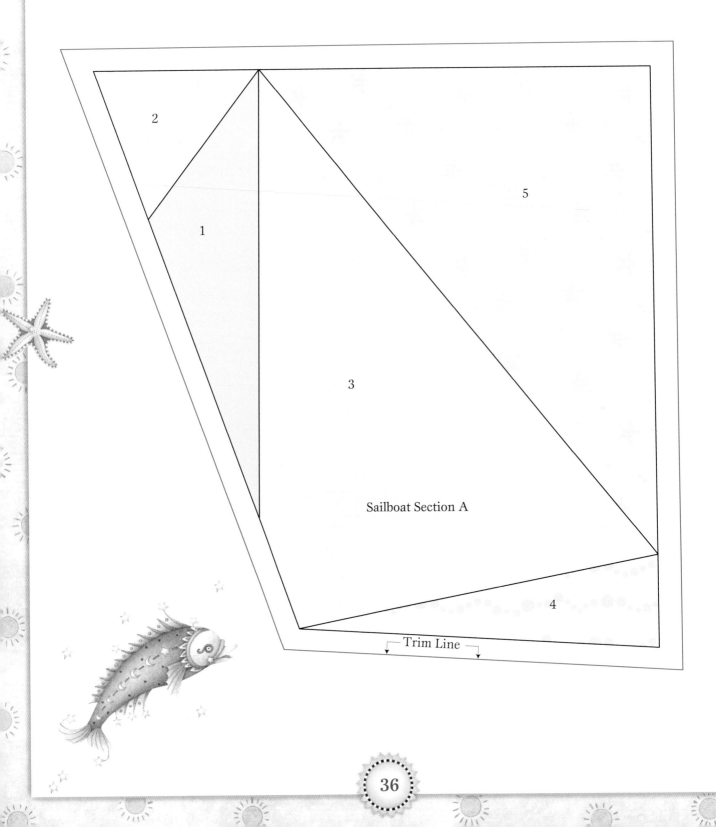

Sailboat Section A

Trim Line

Sailboat Section C

Trim Line

2

1

3

3

Sailboat Section B

2

1

3

Trim Line

Patri✹tic Pinwheels
Lap Quilt

Show your patriotism and set off a shower of visual fireworks with this sparkling match of pinwheels and stars. Declare your independence from template methods with our nifty shortcuts, including quick corner triangles, speedy strip piecing, and efficient big stitch quilting. This quilt is so quick and easy you'll have plenty of time for parades and picnics!

Fabric Requirements and Cutting Instructions

Read all instructions before beginning and use 1/4"-wide seam allowances throughout. Read Cutting the Strips and Pieces on page 78 prior to cutting fabrics.

Patriotic Pinwheels Lap Quilt 49" x 75"	FIRST CUT		SECOND CUT	
	Number of Strips or Pieces	Dimensions	Number of Pieces	Dimensions
☐ Fabric A Background 2 1/8 yards	3	6 1/2" x 42"	14	6 1/2" squares
	2	4 1/4" x 42"	14	4 1/4" squares
	9	3 1/2" x 42"	32	3 1/2" x 6 1/2"
			32	3 1/2" squares
	7	1 1/4" x 42"	14	1 1/4" x 16"
▩ Fabric B Pinwheel-in-Star Background 1/6 yard each of eight fabrics	1 each	4 1/4" square		
	1 each	1 1/4" x 16" *We used four blue and four yellow fabrics.*		
■ Fabric C Pinwheel *assorted scraps*	22 total	4 1/4" squares *We used eleven dark and eleven light fabrics.*		
▨ Fabric D Pinwheel 1/8 yard each of twenty-two fabrics*	1 each	3 1/8" x 16" *We used eleven dark and eleven light fabrics.*		
✶ Fabric E Star 1/8 yard each of eight fabrics	1 each	3 1/2" x 42"	8 *of each fabric*	3 1/2" squares
BORDERS				
■ Sashing/ First Border 3/4 yard	14	1 1/2" x 42"	10	1 1/2" x 12 1/2"
			6	1 1/2" x 38 1/2"
⬚ Second Border 1/3 yard	6	1 1/2" x 42"		
■ Outside Border 2/3 yard	6	3 1/2" x 42"		
■ Binding 5/8 yard	7	2 3/4" x 42"		

Backing - 3 1/4 yards
Batting - 56" x 82"
*Option: 1/8 yard of twelve (6 light and 6 dark) Fabric D, cut one 3 1/8" x 42" strip into two 3 1/8" x 16" strips.

Making the Blocks

You'll be making eight Pinwheel-in-Star Blocks and seven Pinwheel Four-Patch Blocks. All blocks measure 12 1/2" unfinished. Whenever possible, use the Assembly Line Method on page 78. Press in the direction of arrows.

Pinwheel Units

You'll be making a total of twenty-two Pinwheel units: fourteen of Pinwheel A (for Pinwheel Four-Patch blocks) and eight of Pinwheel B (for Pinwheel-in-Star blocks).

1. For Pinwheel A, place 4 1/4" Fabric A square, right sides together, with 4 1/4" Fabric C square. With Fabric A on top, cut twice diagonally. Sew along one short side of each pair. Make four triangle units. Press. Repeat to make fourteen sets of four.

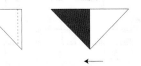

Make 4 matching triangle units
Repeat to make 14 sets

2. Sew 3 1/8" x 16" Fabric D strips and 1 1/4" x 16" Fabric A strips in pairs to make fourteen strip sets. Press. Using rotary cutter and ruler, cut four 3 7/8" segments from each strip set. Set remaining 3 1/8" x 16" Fabric D strips aside for later use.

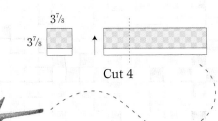

Cut 4

3. Cut each 3⅞" segment from step 2 in half once diagonally to make two triangles. The triangles labeled * will be used to complete the blocks.

*Use this triangle

4. Sew triangle units from step 1 to * triangle units from step 3 (in matching sets of four) along their long edges. Press. If necessary, square units to measure 3½". Make four matching units. Repeat to make fourteen sets of four.

Make 4 matching units
Repeat to make 14 sets
Trim to 3½" square

5. Sew matching units from step 4 together in pairs as shown. Press. Make two. Repeat to make fourteen sets.

Make 2
Repeat to make 14 sets

6. Sew matching units from step 5 together in pairs as shown. Press. Make fourteen and label Pinwheel A. Each unit measures 6½".

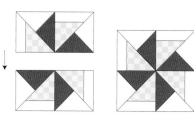

Make 14 of Pinwheel A
Block measures 6½" square

7. For Pinwheel B units, repeat steps 1 through 6 substituting Fabric B for Fabric A. Make thirty-two triangle units (in matching sets of four) and eight strip sets, for a total of eight pinwheel units. Label these blocks Pinwheel B.

Make 8 of Pinwheel B

Pinwheel Four-Patch Blocks

You'll be making a total of seven Pinwheel Four-Patch blocks. Use Pinwheel A units to complete the blocks.

1. Sew each Pinwheel A unit to a 6½" Fabric A square as shown. Press. Make fourteen.

6½

6½

Make 14

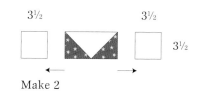

2. Sew two units from step 1 together as shown. Press. Make seven. Block measures 12½" square.

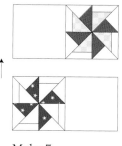

Make 7

Pinwheel-in-Star Blocks

You'll be making eight Pinwheel-in-Star blocks. Use the Pinwheel B units for the center of each star.

1. Refer to Quick Corner Triangle directions on page 78. Sew two matching 3½" Fabric E squares to a 3½" x 6½" Fabric A piece as shown. Press. Make four.

E = 3½ x 3½
A = 3½ x 6½
Make 4

2. Sew a unit from step 1 between two matching 3½" Fabric A squares. Press. Make two.

3½

3½

3½

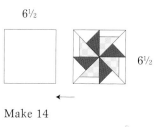

Make 2

3. Sew one Pinwheel B unit between two units from step 1. Press.

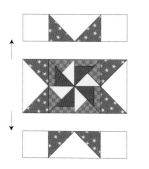

4. Sew unit from step 3 between two units from step 2. Press. Repeat steps 1-4 to make eight blocks. Block measures 12½" square.

Make 8
Block measures 12½" square

Fabric Pinwheels

As much fun as the Fourth of July! Show your colors with these dimensional fabric pinwheels. Perfect for a picnic centerpiece, these star-studded patriotic pinwheels will add a touch of Americana to your décor.

Materials Needed
Pinwheel fabric - scraps
1/4" Dowels
Acrylic paint - blue
Heavyweight fusible web - ½ yard
Buttons - Mill Hill 43015 (optional)

Assembly
1. *For each pinwheel, cut one 6" square of two contrasting fabrics.*
2. *Apply fusible web to each square following manufacturer's instructions.*
3. *Remove paper from fabrics. Fuse two contrasting squares together.*
4. *Draw two diagonal lines. Measure from outside point toward center mark 3¾", this is your cutting "stop" point. Repeat for all sides. Cut along drawn lines stopping at the 3¾" mark.*

5. *Insert threaded needle from the back through center of fabric. Bring every other point toward center inserting needle through the fabric point. After four points are on needle, tack in place. Sew button to center.*
6. *Paint dowel with two coats of acrylic paint. Dry thoroughly.*
7. *To attach Pinwheel to dowel, take a stitch through back of pinwheel and loop thread around dowel. Repeat this process several times, being sure to stitch through fabric each time. Pinwheel will be stationary.*

See page 43 for Patriotic Pot painting instructions.

6

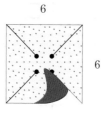

6

Buttons:
Mill Hill/Gay Bowles Sales, Inc.
(800) 356-9438
www.millhill.com

Assembly

1. Arrange two Pinwheel-in-Star blocks, one Pinwheel Four-Patch block, and two 1¹/₂" x 12¹/₂" Sashing/First Border strips to make a horizontal row as shown. Sew blocks and sashing strips together. Press. Make three rows.

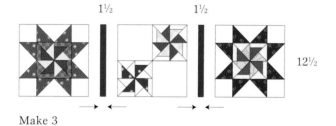

1½   1½

12½

Make 3

2. Arrange two Pinwheel Four-Patch blocks, one Pinwheel-in-Star block, and two 1¹/₂" x 12¹/₂" Sashing/First Border strips to make a horizontal row as shown. Sew blocks and strips together. Press. Make two rows.

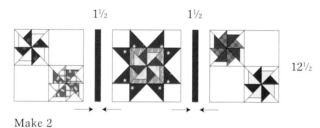

1½   1½

12½

Make 2

3. Refer to color photo on page 38 and layout. Arrange alternating rows from steps 1 and 2, and six 1¹/₂" x 38¹/₂" Sashing/First Border strips. Sew strips and rows together. Press seams toward sashing.

4. Sew remaining 1¹/₂"-wide Sashing/First Border strips together in pairs. Press. Cut two 1¹/₂" x 66¹/₂" strips and sew to sides of quilt. Press.

Big Stitch Quilting Technique

If you plan to combine machine quilting and the Big Stitch Technique, complete machine quilting first. To make a Big Stitch, use embroidery needle with number 8 crochet thread, perle cotton, or three strands of embroidery floss. Anchor knot in the batting as in quilting. Make ¹/₄"-long stitches on top of quilt and ¹/₈"-long stitches under quilt, so large stitches stand out.

Borders

1. Sew 1¹/₂"-wide Second Border strips end to end to make one continuous 1¹/₂"-wide strip. Measure quilt through center from side to side. Trim Second Border strips to that measurement. Sew to top and bottom of quilt. Press seams toward border.

2. Measure quilt through center from top to bottom including borders just added. Cut two strips to that measurement. Sew to sides. Press.

3. Repeat steps 1 and 2 to join, fit, trim, and sew 3¹/₂"-wide Outside Border strips to top, bottom, and sides of quilt. Press seams toward border.

Star Big Stitch Quilting Template

Layering and Finishing

1. Cut backing crosswise into two equal pieces. Sew pieces together to make one 58" x 84" (approximate) backing piece. Arrange and baste backing, batting, and top together, referring to Layering the Quilt directions on page 80.

2. Hand or machine quilt as desired. In our sample, plain squares in the Pinwheel Four-Patch blocks are quilted with the Big Stitch Quilting Technique, using the template at left.

3. Sew 2¾"-wide Binding strips end to end to make one continuous 2¾"-wide strip. Press. Refer to Binding the Quilt on page 80 and bind quilt to finish.

Patriotic Pinwheels Lap Quilt

Finished Size: 49" x 75"
Photo: page 38

Patriotic Pot

Add a splash of color to porch or patio with this easy painting project!

Materials Needed

Terra cotta flowerpot
Acrylic paints in bright red, red/brown, ivory, light tan, medium blue, black, and gold
Assorted paintbrushes
Gesso
Small star stencil/stencil brush
Sea sponge
Note: Allow paint to dry thoroughly after each paint application.

Paint flowerpot with gesso to prepare the surface for painting. Paint lower portion of flowerpot bright red and allow to dry. Dampen sea sponge with water then wring thoroughly. Dip sea sponge in red/ brown paint, blot on a paper towel, then lightly sponge over bright red paint to achieve a mottled effect. When dry, use red/brown paint mixed with black to paint on swirls using a liner brush.

Paint rim of flowerpot with ivory paint. Using a damp sea sponge, sponge light tan over the ivory. Using star stencil and stencil brush, stencil gold stars randomly onto ivory/tan area. Use red paint on a fine brush to add some definition to the stars, then paint a black dot in center of each star.

Paint medium blue on top edge of flowerpot and on the inside. When flowerpot is thoroughly dry, spray with several coats of matte spray varnish to seal. For outside use, use an exterior varnish for more protection.

Finished Size: 50" x 50"

Great Outdoors
Wall Quilt

With its rich, masculine color scheme and delightfully rustic appliqués, this summery quilt is made-to-order for the special outdoorsman in your life. Can't you just picture it in a warm, fire-lit den or as the centerpiece for a cozy, country cabin? It will remind you of outdoor summer adventures all year long!

Fabric Requirements and Cutting Instructions

Read all instructions before beginning and use 1/4"-wide seam allowances throughout. Read Cutting the Strips and Pieces on page 78 prior to cutting fabrics.

Great Outdoors Wall Quilt 50" x 50"	FIRST CUT		SECOND CUT	
	Number of Strips or Pieces	Dimensions	Number of Pieces	Dimensions
Fabric A Background *5/8 yard*	3	5⅞" x 42"	16	5⅞" squares cut once diagonally
Fabric B Block Border & Half Square Triangles *5/8 yard*	2 4	6" x 42" 2" x 42"	8	6" squares
Fabric C Block Border *1/3 yard*	4	2" x 42"		
Fabric D Center Square *1/3 yard*	1	8½" x 42"	4	8½" squares
Fabric E Corner Squares *1/4 yard*	2	3½" x 42"	16	3½" squares
Fabric F Half Square Triangles *3/8 yard*	2	6" x 42"	8	6" squares
BORDERS				
First Border *5/8 yard cut on bias* *1/4 yard is needed for straight cuts*	1	1½"-wide bias strips cut from 18" square		
Second Border *1/4 yard*	5	1" x 42"		
Outside Border *1⅝ yards* *5/8 yard for non-directional fabric*	5	3½" x 42"		
Binding *3/4 yard cut on bias* *1/2 yard is needed for straight cuts*	1	2¾"-wide bias strips cut from 26" square		

Backing - 3⅛ yards
Batting - 56" x 56"
Appliqués - Assorted scraps
Lightweight fusible web - 1/2 yard
Embroidery floss

Making the Blocks

You'll be making four large Square-within-a-Square blocks, two of each variation, to frame the appliqués. All blocks measure 20½" unfinished. Whenever possible, use the Assembly Line Method on page 78. Press in the direction of arrows.

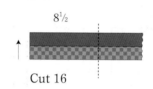

1. Sew 2" x 42" Fabric B strips and 2" x 42" Fabric C strips together lengthwise in pairs. Press. Cut into sixteen 8½" segments.

8½

Cut 16

2. Sew each 8½" Fabric D square between two segments from step 1 as shown. Press. Make two of each variation.

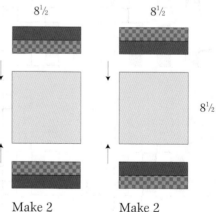

Make 2   Make 2

3. Sew each remaining segment from step 1 between two 3½" Fabric E squares as shown. Press. Make eight.

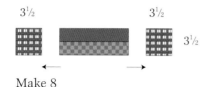

3½   3½

3½

Make 8

4. Sew each unit from step 2 between two units from step 3 as shown. Press. Make two of each variation.

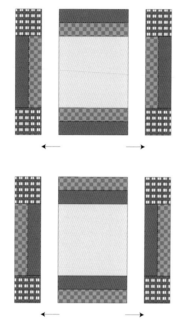

Make 2 of each variation

5. Make Half-Square Triangles by drawing a diagonal line on wrong side of 6" Fabric B square. Place marked 6" Fabric B square and 6" Fabric F square right sides together. Sew scant 1/4" from both sides of drawn line as shown. Make eight. Cut on drawn line. Press eight seams toward Fabric B and eight toward Fabric F. Trim to 5½". This will make sixteen half-square triangles.

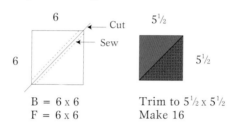

6   5½
             Cut
             Sew
6   5½

B = 6 x 6   Trim to 5½ x 5½
F = 6 x 6   Make 16

6. Sew each unit from step 5 to Fabric A triangle along the triangle's short side as shown. (Note: Triangle will extend past raw edge of square. For clarity, seam allowances are shown on diagrams 6-9.) Press. Make sixteen.

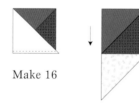

Make 16

7. Sew remaining Fabric A triangles to each unit from step 6 along the triangle's short side as shown. Press. Make sixteen.

Make 16

8. Sew each unit from step 4 between two units from step 7 as shown. (Note: Triangle will extend past raw edge of square.) Press. Make four.

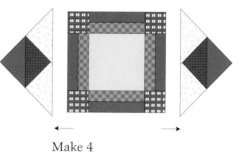

Make 4

9. Sew each unit from step 8 between units from step 7 as shown. Press. Make four. Block measures 20½" square.

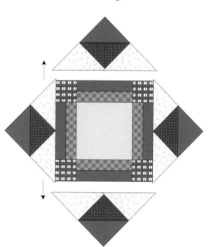

Make 4
Block measures 20½" square

Assembly

1. Refer to the quilt layout on page 48 and the color photo on page 44. Lay out the four large Square-within-a-Square blocks in two rows of two blocks each, taking care to position them as shown. Sew blocks together in pairs. Press seams in opposite directions from row to row.

2. Sew rows together. Press.

Borders

1. We used bias strips for the First Border. Refer to Making Bias Strips on page 78. Start with an 18" square to cut bias strips. You will need approximately 170" of 1½"-wide bias strip (if you prefer to make a straight cut border instead, cut five 1½" x 42" strips).

2. Measure quilt through center from side to side. Trim two bias strips to that measurement. Sew to top and bottom. Press seams toward border.

3. Measure quilt through center from top to bottom, including borders just added. Trim two 1½"-wide pieced bias strips to that measurement. Sew to sides. Press.

4. Sew 1" x 42" Second Border strips end to end to make one continuous 1"-wide strip. Press. Repeat steps 2 and 3 to fit, trim, and sew 1"-wide Second Border strips to top, bottom, and sides. Press seams toward border.

5. If using directional fabric, cut two lengthwise and three crosswise (pieced) strips. Sew to top, bottom, and sides of quilt. If using non-directional fabric, repeat step 4 to join, fit, trim, and sew 3½"-wide Outside Border strips to top, bottom, and sides. Press.

Great Outdoors Accessories

Bring the great outdoors inside with these easy home décor projects.

Add light and personality to your home with this fun and easy lamp project. A jar lid adapter converts a plain canning jar into a lamp base filled with walk-in-the-woods finds. Simply fill the canning jar with found objects, then screw on the lamp adapter. Available at craft stores, adapters are generally a brass color, so we painted ours light green to accent items in the jar. Add a purchased lampshade and your lamp is ready for use.

Note: Make sure all items are thoroughly dried before placing in jar.

This woodsy picture frame is easily constructed using scrapbooking stickers and punch-outs. Simply embellish a purchased acid-free double mat with border stickers and add thematic stickers and punch-outs along the bottom edge. For dimensional tree and bear, apply stickers to a piece of self-adhesive photo mat and cut around stickers with a craft knife. Attach to mat with adhesive. Place picture in the frame and use adhesive to adhere a piece of acid-free mat board as a backing. Wrap a sticker border around edges to finish.

Adding the Appliqués

The instructions given are for quick-fuse appliqué. If you prefer traditional hand appliqué, be sure to reverse all appliqué templates and add ¼"-wide seam allowances when cutting appliqué pieces. Refer to Hand Appliqué on page 79.

1. Refer to Quick-Fuse Appliqué on page 79. Trace appliqué patterns on pages 49-51 for fish, moose, lodge, kayak, and oar.

2. Refer to quilt layout below and color photo on page 44 to position appliqués on blocks. Fuse appliqués in place and finish with machine satin stitch or decorative stitching as desired.

3. Refer to Embroidery Stitch Guide on page 78 and color photo on page 44. Use two strands of embroidery floss and a colonial knot to embroider an eye for moose and cabin doorknob, and a satin stitch to embroider an eye for fish. Or, use small buttons for doorknob and eyes.

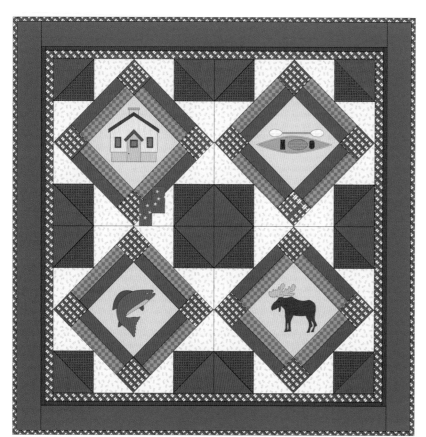

Great Outdoors Wall Quilt

Finished Size: 50" x 50"
Photo: page 44

Layering and Finishing

1. Cut backing crosswise into two equal pieces. Sew pieces together to make one 56" x 84" (approximate) backing piece. Trim to 56" x 56". Arrange and baste backing, batting, and top together referring to Layering the Quilt directions on page 80.

2. Hand or machine quilt as desired.

3. We used bias strips for our binding. Refer to Making Bias Strips on page 78. Start with a 26" square to cut bias strips. You will need approximately 205" of 2¾"-wide bias binding strips. If you prefer to make a straight cut binding instead of bias, cut six 2¾" x 42" strips. Refer to Binding the Quilt on page 80 and bind quilt to finish.

Tracing Line _____

Tracing Line - - - - - - - - - -
(will be hidden behind other fabrics)

Tracing Line _____
Tracing Line _ _ _ _ _ _ _ _ _ _
(will be hidden behind other fabrics)

Tracing Line _____
Tracing Line _ _ _ _ _ _ _ _ _ _ _
(will be hidden behind other fabrics)

Finished Size: 37" x 37"

Autumn Glory
Wall Quilt

*Tumbled leaves and earthy acorns
complement the colorful quail showcased
in the center of this charming,
medallion-style wall quilt. A cadre of
quick-pieced flying geese provide a fitting frame,
while shimmering stalks of harvest wheat,
worked in a variety of textural embroidery
stitches, add the just-right finishing touch.*

Fabric Requirements and Cutting Instructions

Read all instructions before beginning and use 1/4"-wide seam allowances throughout. Read Cutting the Strips and Pieces on page 78 prior to cutting fabrics.

Autumn Glory Wall Quilt 37" x 37"	FIRST CUT		SECOND CUT	
	Number of Strips or Pieces	Dimensions	Number of Pieces	Dimensions
Fabric A Background *1/2 yard*	1	15 1/2" square		
Fabric B Flying Geese *Assorted scraps or 1/6 yard*	16	4 1/2" x 2 1/2"		
Fabric C Flying Geese Background *1/3 yard*	3	2 1/2" x 42"	36	2 1/2" squares
Fabric D Accent Border *1/8 yard*	2	1" x 42"	2 2	1" x 15 1/2" 1" x 16 1/2"
Fabric E 1st and 5th Borders *1/3 yard**	6	1 1/2" x 42"*		
Fabric F 2nd and 4th Borders *1/3 yard**	6	1 1/2" x 42"*		
Fabric G Corners *Scrap*	4	2 1/2" squares		
Fabric H Maple Leaves *Assorted scraps or 1/4 yard*	4 20	2 1/2" x 4 1/2" 2 1/2" squares		
Fabric I Maple Leaf Background *1/4 yard*	2	2 1/2" x 42"	20 8	2 1/2" squares 2 1/4" squares
Fabric J Leaf Stems *Scraps*	4	2 1/2" squares		
Fabric K 3rd Border *5/8 yard*	4	4 1/2" x 42"		
Binding *3/8 yard*	4	2 3/4" x 42"		

Backing - 1 1/6 yards*
Batting - 42" x 42"
Quail, leaf, acorn appliqués - Assorted scraps
Lightweight fusible web - 1/2 yard
Embroidery floss
Silk ribbon (4mm and 5mm) - 3 yards each
Bead for quail eye
*Fabric must measure 42" or wider

Assembling the Quilt Center

Whenever possible, use the Assembly Line Method on page 78. Press in the direction of arrows.

1. Sew 1" x 15 1/2" Fabric D strips to top and bottom of 15 1/2" Fabric A square. Press seams toward strips. Repeat to sew two 1" x 16 1/2" Fabric D strips to sides. Press.

2. Referring to Quick Corner Triangles on page 78, sew two 2 1/2" Fabric C squares to each 4 1/2" x 2 1/2" Fabric B piece as shown. Press. Make sixteen.

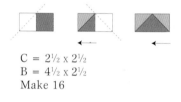

C = 2 1/2 x 2 1/2
B = 4 1/2 x 2 1/2
Make 16

3. Arrange four units from step 2 to make a horizontal row as shown. Sew units together. Press seams open. Make four rows.

Make 4

4. Sew a unit from step 3 between two 2 1/2" Fabric C squares. Press. Make two.

2 1/2   2 1/2

2 1/2

Make 2

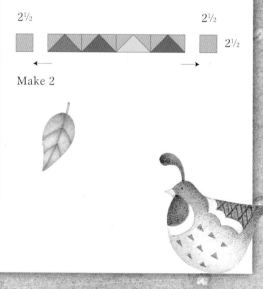

5. Sew unit from step 1 between two units from step 3. Press seams toward center. Repeat to sew units from step 4 to sides. Press. Block measures 20½" square.

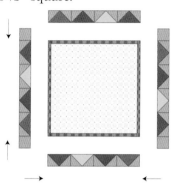

Block measures 20½" square

6. Sew 1½" x 42" Fabric E strip and 1½" x 42" Fabric F strip together lengthwise to make a strip set. Press. Make two strip sets. Cut into four 2½" x 20½" segments.

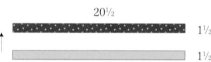

7. Refer to layout on page 56 and color photo on page 52. Sew unit from step 5 between two border units from step 6, taking care to position border units as shown. Press toward border units.

8. Sew each remaining border unit from step 6 between two 2½" Fabric G squares. Press seams toward border units. Make two.

9. Sew border units from step 8 to sides of unit from step 7. Press toward border units.

Maple Leaf Blocks

1. Making quick corner triangle units, sew 2½" Fabric H and 2½" Fabric I squares together in pairs as shown. Trim and press. Make sixteen.

H = 2½ x 2½
I = 2½ x 2½
Make 16

2. Making quick corner triangle units, sew 2¼" Fabric I square to opposite corners of each 2½" Fabric J square as shown. Press. Make four.

I = 2¼ x 2¼
J = 2½ x 2½
Make 4

3. Sew remaining 2½" Fabric H squares and units from step 2 together in pairs. Press. Make four.

2½

2½

Make 4

4. Sew 2½" x 4½" Fabric H pieces and units from step 3 together in pairs as shown. Press. Make four.

4½

2½

Make 4

5. Sew eight units from step 1 together in pairs as shown. Press. Make four.

Make 4

6. Sew unit from step 5 and unit from step 4 together as shown. Press. Make four.

Make 4

7. Sew remaining 2½" Fabric I squares and remaining units from step 1 together as shown. Press. Make four.

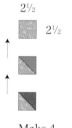

2½

2½

Make 4

8. Sew a unit from step 7 to each unit from step 6 as shown. Press. Make four.

Make 4

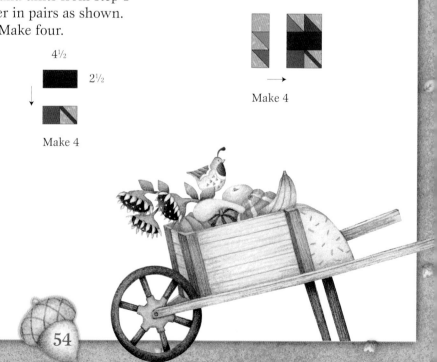

Borders

1. Sew 4½" x 42" Fabric K strip, 1½" x 42" Fabric F strip, and 1½" x 42" Fabric E strip in order shown to make a strip set. Press. Make four strip sets.

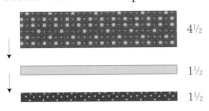

4½

1½

1½

2. Measure quilt through center from side to side, and from top to bottom. (These measurements should be the same). Trim four border units to this measurement from the strip sets created in step 1.

3. Referring to quilt layout on page 56, sew quilt top between two border units from step 2, taking care to position border units as shown. Press toward border units.

4. Sew each remaining border unit from step 2 between two Maple Leaf blocks as shown. Press. Make two.

Make 2

5. Sew border units from step 4 to sides of unit from step 3. Press.

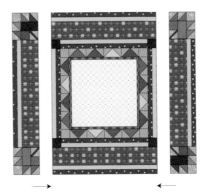

Adding the Appliqués

The instructions given are for the Quick-Fuse Appliqué method. If you prefer traditional hand appliqué, be sure to reverse all appliqué templates and add ¼" seam allowances when cutting appliqué pieces. Refer to Hand Appliqué directions on page 79.

1. Referring to Quick-Fuse Appliqué on page 79, trace appliqué patterns on pages 56-57 for quail, leaves, and acorns.

2. Referring to quilt layout on page 56 and color photo on page 52, position appliqués on blocks. Fuse appliqués in place and finish with machine satin stitch or decorative stitching as desired.

Autumn Glory Table Topper

Bring the colors and seasonal symbols of autumn to your table with this bountiful table topper.

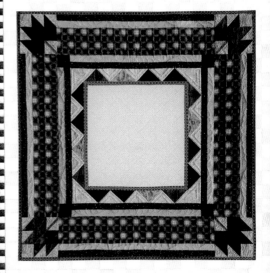

Beautiful in bright colors or sophisticated in more subtle hues, this table topper will set the scene for sumptuous harvest suppers.

Construction of the table topper is identical to the Autumn Glory Wall Quilt, simply omit the appliqués in the center of the medallion. The table topper provides the perfect setting for a handsome harvest centerpiece. See photo on page 58.

Layering and Finishing

1. Referring to Layering the Quilt on page 80, arrange and baste backing, batting, and top together.

2. Hand or machine quilt as desired.

3. Refer to Binding the Quilt directions on page 80 and use 2³/₄"-wide strips for binding.

4. Refer to Embroidery Stitch Guide on page 78 and color photo on page 52. Use silk ribbon and a lazy daisy stitch to embroider the wheat kernels. Use three strands of embroidery floss and a stem stitch to embroider feathers on the quail's wing, leaf veins, and wheat stalks. Use a running stitch to embroider wheat beards. Attach bead for quail eye.

Wheat
Embroidery
Template

Autumn Glory Wall Quilt

Finished Size: 37" x 37"
Photo: page 52

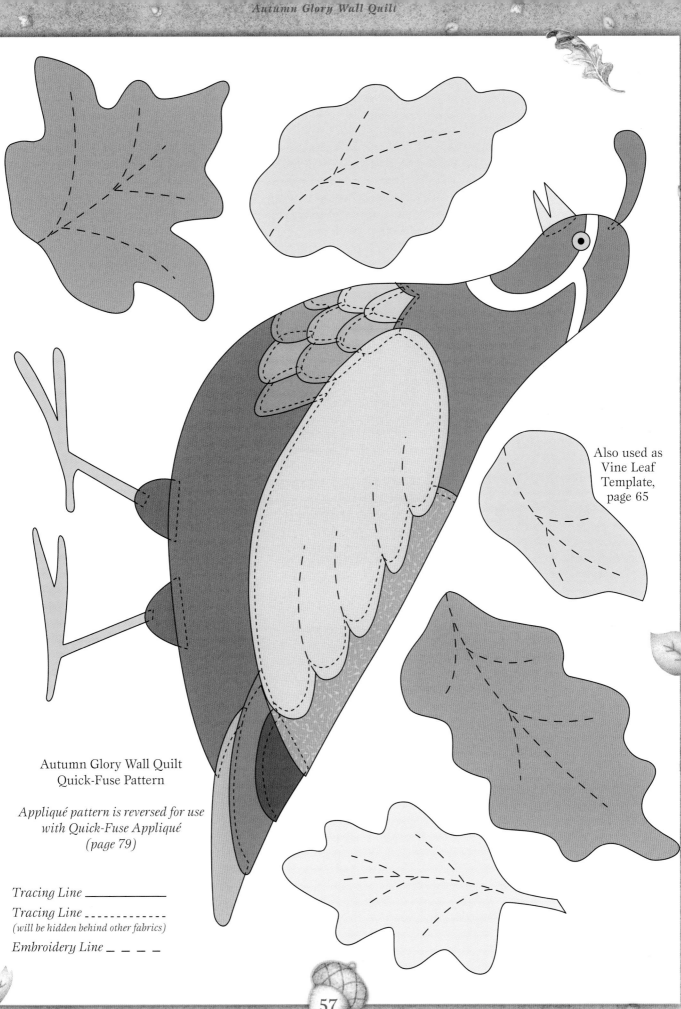

Also used as
Vine Leaf
Template,
page 65

Autumn Glory Wall Quilt
Quick-Fuse Pattern

*Appliqué pattern is reversed for use
with Quick-Fuse Appliqué
(page 79)*

Tracing Line _____

Tracing Line _ _ _ _ _ _ _ _
(will be hidden behind other fabrics)

Embroidery Line _ _ _ _

Harvest Celebration
Centerpiece

The abundance of the harvest is celebrated with this radiant centerpiece overflowing with the fruits and vegetables of autumn. The rich hues and subtle textures of the season inspired the simple, yet sensational, painting technique for the pedestal bowl. Gourds, grapes, wheat, leaves, acorns, and other gifts from nature fill the bowl to overflowing.

Materials Needed

Terra cotta hanging planter
Terra cotta flowerpot saucer
Gesso
Acrylic paints in paprika,
    medium green, ivory,
    light gold, brown, purple,
    medium gray, and black
Crackle medium
Antiquing medium
Assorted paintbrushes
Sea sponge
Wooden plugs
Fruits, vegetables, wheat, leaves,
and other natural products

Painting the Pedestal Bowl

We used a decorative terra cotta hanging planter as the pedestal base for the centerpiece and a flowerpot saucer to form the bowl. When purchasing supplies, look for a planter with interesting details. Turn the planter upside down and try several sizes of saucers to select the most visually appealing. If using a hanging planter, remove chain and fill holes by gluing on wooden plugs. The planter and saucer shown were purchased at a major home improvement store.

Determine the placement of each paint color using the details of your planter and saucer as the guide. General instructions for our centerpiece can serve as your painting guide. All instructions are written assuming the planter is turned upside down to form the pedestal.
Note: Allow paint to dry thoroughly between each paint application.

1. Using a paintbrush, apply gesso to clean, dry, terra cotta planter and saucer to prepare the surfaces.

2. Paint the lower portions of pedestal and saucer with brown paint. Allow to dry.

3. Following manufacturer's directions, apply crackle medium over brown paint in a very thin coat on each piece and allow to "set". Apply a quick, even coat of paprika paint to the same areas. Crackles will appear in the painted surfaces. Do not touch as surface is very fragile when wet. Allow to dry thoroughly.

4. Using details of the saucer as your guide, paint a purple stripe on saucer and apply black paint on the rim and interior of the saucer. When dry, use a slightly damp sea sponge and a tapping motion to sponge medium gray paint over the black. Use a light touch to get a slightly mottled effect. Apply light gold paint to center section of pedestal. When dry, sponge ivory paint over the light gold. Use a light touch to blend colors.

5. Using details of your pedestal, paint stripes with medium green and purple.

6. When paint has dried thoroughly, apply a coat of matte spray varnish.

7. Follow manufacturer's directions to apply antiquing medium to both pieces. When dry, spray pedestal and saucer with several coats of matte spray varnish.

8. Center saucer on pedestal and fill with faux or real fruits, vegetables, leaves, nuts, etc. To make storage easier, do not permanently attach the saucer to the pedestal. Each piece can also be used independently for other decorating uses.

Finished Size: 28" x 50"

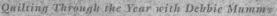

Happy Harvest
Door Banner

Warmly welcome your autumn guests with this clever and colorful harvest door banner. Overflowing with a bounty of seasonal symbols, it's sure to please even the littlest hobgoblin. Best of all, our time-saving piecing "tricks" make construction a "treat"!

Fabric Requirements and Cutting Instructions

Read all instructions before beginning and use ¼"-wide seam allowances throughout. Read Cutting the Strips and Pieces on page 78 prior to cutting fabrics.

Happy Harvest Door Banner 28" x 50"	FIRST CUT		SECOND CUT	
	Number of Strips or Pieces	Dimensions	Number of Pieces	Dimensions
Fabric A Corn & Pumpkin Background ½ yard	1	2½" x 42"	3	2½" x 5½"
	7	1½" x 42"	1	1½" x 17½"
			2	1½" x 14½"
			1	1½" x 12½"
			3	1½" x 10½"
			3	1½" x 7½"
			6	1½" x 5½"
			10	1½" x 2¾"
			33	1½" squares
Fabric B Flying Geese, Leaves, & Feathers *assorted scraps to equal 1½ yards*		Flying Geese	19 total	2½" x 4½"
			38 total	2½" squares
		Feathers	6 total	4½" squares
		Maple Leaves	4 total	2½" x 6½"
			4 total	2½" x 4½"
			8 total	2½" squares
Fabric C Corn Stalk, Pumpkin Stems, & Row Borders ¼ yard	4	1½" x 42"	1	1½" x 30½"
			3	1½" x 12½"
			4	1½" x 8½"
			1	1½" x 5½"
			5	1½" squares
			5	1½" x 1"
Fabric D Leaf & Feather Background ⅙ yard each of two fabrics	1*	2½" x 42"	16*	2½" squares
	4*	2¼" squares		
		cut for each fabric		
Fabric E Leaf Stems *scraps*	4	2½" squares		
Fabric F, G, H, and I Stripes ⅛ yard each color		Fabric F Stripe	1	2½" x 24"
		Fabric G Stripe	1	1½" x 24"
		Fabric H Stripe	1	2" x 24"
		Fabric I Stripe	1	2" x 24"
Fabric J Pumpkins *scraps*	3	4½" x 5½"		
	2	3½" x 5½"		
BORDERS				
Accent Border ⅙ yard	4	1" x 42"		
Outside Border ½ yard	4	3" x 42"		
Binding ⅔ yard cut on bias OR ⅜ yard for straight cut		2¾"-wide bias strips cut from 23" square		

Vine Leaves - Assorted scraps
Yellow silk ribbon (4mm) - 3 yards
Backing - 1⅝ yards

Batting - 35" x 57"
Green perle cotton

Making the Units and Blocks

You'll be making nineteen Flying Geese Units, one Cornstalk Block, six Feather Blocks, two Stripe Units, four Maple Leaf Blocks, and a total of five Pumpkin Blocks in two different sizes. Whenever possible, use the Assembly Line Method on page 78. Press in the direction of arrows.

Flying Geese Units

Refer to Quick Corner Triangle directions on page 78. Sew two matching 2½" Fabric B squares to a contrasting 2½" x 4½" Fabric B piece as shown. Press. Make nineteen.

B = 2½ x 2½
B = 2½ x 4½
Make 19

Cornstalk Block

1. Refer to Quick Corner Triangle directions on page 78. Sew two 1½" Fabric A squares to each 1½" x 8½" Fabric C piece as shown. Make two of each variation.

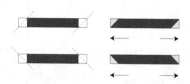

A = 1½ x 1½
C = 1½ x 8½
Make 2 of each variation

2. Making quick corner triangle units, sew 1½" Fabric A squares and 1½" Fabric C squares together in pairs. Press. Make five.

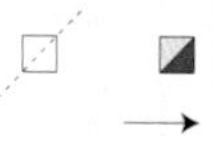

A = 1½ x 1½
C = 1½ x 1½
Make 5

3. Refer to the layout on page 65 and the color photo on page 60. Arrange the 1¹/₂" x 5¹/₂" Fabric A pieces, 1¹/₂" x 14¹/₂" Fabric A strips, 1¹/₂" x 17¹/₂" Fabric A strip, 1¹/₂" x 7¹/₂" Fabric A pieces, 1¹/₂" x 10¹/₂" Fabric A pieces, 1¹/₂" x 12¹/₂" Fabric A piece, 1¹/₂" x 30¹/₂" Fabric C strip, and the units from steps 1 and 2 as shown.

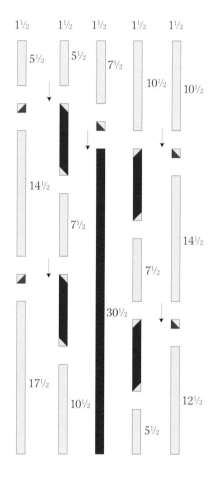

4. Sew pieces, strips, and units into five vertical rows. Press seams toward Fabric A strips, except where noted by arrows.

5. Sew rows together. Press seams toward center. Section B is now complete and measures 5¹/₂" x 38¹/₂".

Feather Blocks

1. Refer to Quick Corner Triangle directions on page 78. Sew two 2¹/₂" Fabric D squares to a 4¹/₂" Fabric B square as shown. Press. Make six.

D = 2¹/₂ x 2¹/₂
B = 4¹/₂ x 4¹/₂
Make 6

2. Arrange and sew three units from step 1 to make two horizontal rows as shown. Press.

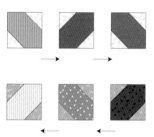

Stripe Units

1. Sew the 2¹/₂" x 24" Fabric F strip, 1¹/₂" x 24" Fabric G strip, 2" x 24" Fabric H strip, and 2" x 24" Fabric I strip in the order shown to make a strip set. Press. Cut four 5¹/₂" segments.

24

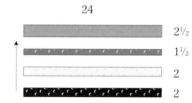

2¹/₂
1¹/₂
2
2

5¹/₂

Cut 4

Sew two segments from step 1 together to make stripe units as shown. Press. Make 2.

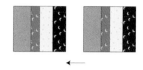

Maple Leaf Blocks

You will be making four Maple Leaves, each a different color.

1. Refer to Quick Corner Triangle directions on page 78. Sew one 2¹/₂" Fabric D square to one 2¹/₂" Fabric B square. Press. Make two for each Maple Leaf.

D = 2¹/₂ x 2¹/₂
B = 2¹/₂ x 2¹/₂
Make 2 per leaf

2. Sew one 2¹/₂" Fabric D square and two units from step 1 together as shown. Press. Make one for each Maple Leaf.

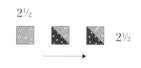

2¹/₂

2¹/₂

3. Making a quick corner triangle unit, sew one 2¹/₂" Fabric D square to one 2¹/₂" x 6¹/₂" Fabric B piece as shown. Press. Make one for each Maple Leaf.

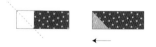

D = 2¹/₂ x 2¹/₂
B = 2¹/₂ x 6¹/₂

4. Making a quick corner triangle unit, sew one 2¹/₂" Fabric D square to one 2¹/₂" x 4¹/₂" Fabric B piece as shown. Press. Make one for each Maple Leaf.

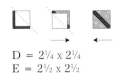

D = 2¹/₂ x 2¹/₂
B = 2¹/₂ x 4¹/₂

5. Making quick corner triangle units, sew one 2¹/₄" Fabric D square to one 2¹/₂" Fabric E square as shown. Press. Repeat to sew one 2¹/₄" Fabric D square to opposite end of unit. Make one for each Maple Leaf. Press.

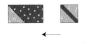

D = 2¹/₄ x 2¹/₄
E = 2¹/₂ x 2¹/₂

6. Sew units from steps 4 and 5 together as shown. Press.

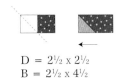

7. Sew units from steps 2, 3, and 6 together as shown. Press. Make four. Refer to layout on page 65 to sew Maple Leaves together in pairs. Press.

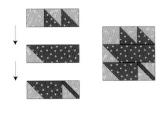

Pumpkin Blocks

1. Refer to Quick Corner Triangle directions on page 78. Sew four 1¹/₂" Fabric A squares to each 3¹/₂" x 5¹/₂" Fabric J piece as shown. Press. Make two.

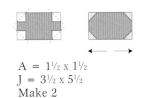

A = 1¹/₂ x 1¹/₂
J = 3¹/₂ x 5¹/₂
Make 2

2. Repeat step 1 to sew four 1¹/₂" Fabric A squares to each 4¹/₂" x 5¹/₂" Fabric J piece as shown. Press. Make three.

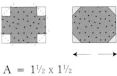

A = 1¹/₂ x 1¹/₂
J = 4¹/₂ x 5¹/₂
Make 3

3. Sew a 1¹/₂" x 1" Fabric C piece between two 1¹/₂" x 2³/₄" Fabric A pieces. Press. Make five.

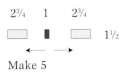

2³/₄   1   2³/₄

1¹/₂

Make 5

4. Sew a unit from step 3 between a 1¹/₂" x 5¹/₂" Fabric A strip and a unit from step 1 as shown. Press. Make two.

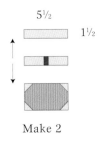

5¹/₂

1¹/₂

Make 2

5. Sew a unit from step 3 to a unit from step 2 as shown. Press. Make three.

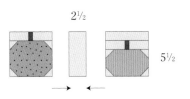

Make 3

6. Sew a 2¹/₂" x 5¹/₂" Fabric A piece between a unit from step 5 and step 4. Press and label Row 4.

2¹/₂

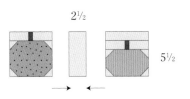

7. Sew a unit from step 5, 1¹/₂" x 5¹/₂" Fabric A piece, 1¹/₂" x 5¹/₂" Fabric C piece, 2¹/₂" x 5¹/₂" Fabric A piece, unit from step 4, 2¹/₂" x 5¹/₂" Fabric A piece, and unit from step 5 in order as shown. Press and label Row 8.

1¹/₂ 1¹/₂ 2¹/₂   2¹/₂

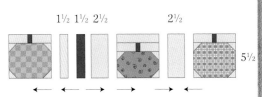

5¹/₂

Assembly

1. Refer to the assembly diagram below and the color photo on page 60. Lay out the Flying Geese Units, Cornstalk Block, Feather Rows, Stripe Units, Maple Leaf Rows, Pumpkin Rows, and 1½" x 12½" Fabric C strips as shown.

2. Sew the Flying Geese Units in a vertical row to complete Section A. Press. Section A measures 4½" x 38½".

3. Sew the Feather Rows, Stripe Units, 1½" x 12½" Fabric C strips, Maple Leaf Rows, and Pumpkin Row 4 to complete Section C. Press. Section C measures 12½" x 38½".

4. Sew Sections A, B, and C together. Press seams toward Section B. Add Pumpkin Row 8 to bottom. Press toward Row 8.

Borders

1. Sew 1"-wide Accent Border strips end to end to make one continuous 1"-wide strip. Measure quilt through center from side to side. Trim two 1"-wide Accent Border strips to that measurement. Sew to top and bottom. Press seams toward border.

2. Measure quilt through center from top to bottom, including borders just added. Trim two 1"-wide Accent Border strips to that measurement from remaining 1"-wide strip. Sew to sides. Press.

3. Sew 3"-wide Outside Border strips end to end to make one continuous 3"-wide strip. Repeat steps 1 and 2 to fit, trim, and sew 3"-wide strips to top, bottom, and sides. Press seams toward border.

Layering and Finishing

1. Cut backing to make one 35" x 57" piece. Arrange and baste backing, batting, and top together, referring to Layering the Quilt directions on page 80.

2. Hand or machine quilt as desired.

3. We used bias strips for our binding. Refer to Making Bias Strips on page 78. Start with a 23" square. You will need approximately 156" of 2¾"-wide bias strips. (For straight cut binding, cut four 2¾" x 42" binding strips). Refer to Binding the Quilt on page 80 to bind quilt to finish.

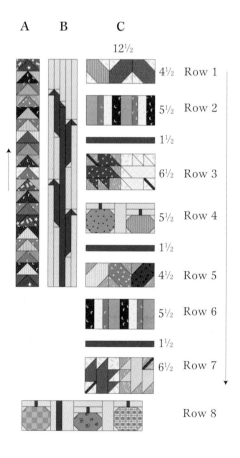

A   B   C

12½

4½ — Row 1
5½ — Row 2
1½
6½ — Row 3
5½ — Row 4
1½
4½ — Row 5
5½ — Row 6
1½
6½ — Row 7
Row 8

Corn Tassel
Embroidery Template

4. Refer to Embroidery Guide on page 78 and quilt layout. Use perle cotton and a stem stitch to embroider vines around pumpkins. Use 4mm silk ribbon and a ribbon stitch to embroider corn tassel.

5. Trace Vine Leaf Template on page 57. Use template to trace desired number of leaves on wrong side of assorted scraps. Place traced leaves with matching fabric right sides together. Sew on traced line. Trim seam allowance to 3/16". Cut a slit in one side of leaf shape and turn right side out. Press. Referring to quilt layout, stitch through leaves lengthwise to attach to quilt.

Happy Harvest Door Banner

Finished Size: 28" x 50"
Photo: page 60

Harvest Table Runner

Bring autumn's bounty to your table with this colorful table runner. The Happy Harvest Door Banner pattern is easily altered to make this charming table decoration.

Finished Size: 19" x 50"

Fabric Requirements

Refer to Happy Harvest Door Banner on page 61 for fabric requirements and cutting instructions for Fabric B (Maple Leaves and Feathers), and Fabrics D, E, F, G, H, and I.

Fabric A Background (1/6 yard)
   two 2 1/2" x 5 1/2" pieces
   two 1 1/2" x 5 1/2" pieces
   eight 1 1/2" x 2 3/4" pieces
   sixteen 1 1/2" squares

Fabric C Pumpkin Stems, Leaves, & Row Borders (1/8 yard)
   three 1 1/2" x 12 1/2" pieces
   four 1 1/2" x 1" pieces

Fabric J Pumpkins (scraps)
   two 4 1/2" x 5 1/2" pieces
   two 3 1/2" x 5 1/2" pieces

Accent Border (1/8 yard)
   three 1" x 42" strips

Outside Border (1/2 yard)
   four 3" x 42" strips

Binding (5/8 yard bias or 3/8 yard straight cut)

Backing - 1 1/2 yards

Batting - 24" x 54"

Perle cotton and silk ribbon

Making the Table Runner

1. Refer to Happy Harvest Door Banner instructions, page 62-63, for making Feather Blocks, Stripe Units, and Maple Leaf Blocks.

2. For Pumpkin Blocks, refer to page 63, and follow step 1, step 2 (making two not three), and step 3 (making four not five). Follow steps 4-6 to complete two pumpkin rows.

3. Refer to table runner layout above to position and sew together Feather Blocks, Stripe Units, three 1 1/2" x 12 1/2" Fabric C strips, Maple Leaf Blocks, and Pumpkin Rows or assemble according to your own preference. Press. Quilt top measures 12 1/2" x 43 1/2".

4. Measure quilt top through center from side to side. Cut two strips to that measurement. Sew to top and bottom of quilt. Sew remaining Accent Border strips end to end to make one continuous 1 1/2"-wide strip. Press. Measure quilt top through center from top to bottom. Cut two Accent Border strips to that measurement and sew to sides of quilt.

5. Repeat step 4 to add 3"-wide Outside Border strips to top, bottom, and sides of quilt.

6. Cut Backing to 23" x 54". Arrange and baste backing, batting, and top together referring to Layering the Quilt on page 80. Hand or machine quilt as desired.

7. For bias binding, refer to Making Bias Strips on page 78. Start with a 20" square. You will need approximately 140" of 2 3/4"-wide bias binding. (For straight cut binding, cut four 2 3/4" x 42" binding strips). Refer to Binding the Quilt on page 80 to bind quilt to finish.

8. Refer to Layering and Finishing at left to embroider quilt and make four Vine Leaves.

Finished Size: 81" x 105"

Foursquare Flannel
Bed Quilt

It may be cold outside, but inside you'll be cozy and warm with this snuggly flannel quilt! Courthouse Square blocks combine with a modified T-Square block to create a Southwestern-style pattern that accentuates the rich colors and soft textures of flannels. Half-square triangles and quick corner triangles make assembly-line construction quick and easy, so you'll have plenty of time to make the matching pillowcases for a complete bed ensemble.

Fabric Requirements and Cutting Instructions

Read all instructions before beginning and use 1/4"-wide seam allowances throughout. Read Cutting the Strips and Pieces on page 78 prior to cutting fabrics.

Foursquare Flannel Bed Quilt 81" x 105"	FIRST CUT		SECOND CUT	
	Number of Strips or Pieces	Dimensions	Number of Pieces	Dimensions
Fabric A Courthouse Center 1/4 yard	2	3 1/2" x 42"	17	3 1/2" squares
Fabric B 1st Light Logs and Block A Triangles 1 1/4 yards	3 6 4	5" x 42" 2 1/2" x 42" 2" x 42"	24 48 34	5" squares 2 1/2" x 4 1/2" 2" x 3 1/2"
Fabric C 1st Dark Logs, Block A Center, and Triangles 1 5/8 yards	2 3 6 6	4 1/2" x 42" 5" x 42" 2 1/2" x 42" 2" x 42"	12 24 96 34	4 1/2" squares 5" squares 2 1/2" squares 2" x 6 1/2"
Fabric D 2nd Light Logs 1/2 yard	6	2" x 42"	34	2" x 6 1/2"
Fabric E 2nd Dark Logs, Block B Triangles, and Rectangles 1 1/3 yards	2 6 9	5" x 42" 2 1/2" x 42" 2" x 42"	12 48 34	5" squares 2 1/2" x 4 1/2" 2" x 9 1/2"
Fabric F 3rd Light Logs 5/8 yard	9	2" x 42"	34	2" x 9 1/2"
Fabric G 3rd Dark Logs 3/4 yard	12	2" x 42"	34	2" x 12 1/2"
Fabric H Block B Triangles 5/8 yard	2 3	5" x 42" 2 1/2" x 42"	12 48	5" squares 2 1/2" squares
Fabric I Block A Rectangles, Block B Centers 5/8 yard	1 6	4 1/2" x 42" 2 1/2" x 42"	6 48	4 1/2" squares 2 1/2" x 4 1/2"
BORDERS				
First Border 1/2 yard	8	1 1/2" x 42"		
Second Border 7/8 yard	8	3 1/2" x 42"		
Outside Border 1 7/8 yards	9	6 1/2" x 42"		
Binding 1 yard		2 3/4" bias strips cut from 34" square		
Backing - 7 3/4 yards Batting - 88" x 112"				

Making the Blocks

You will be making thirty-five blocks: seventeen Courthouse Blocks, twelve Block A, and six Block B. Blocks measure 12 1/2" square unfinished. Whenever possible, use the Assembly Line Method on page 78. Press seams in the direction of the arrows.

Courthouse Blocks

1. Sew a 3 1/2" Fabric A square between two 2" x 3 1/2" Fabric B pieces as shown. Press. Make seventeen.

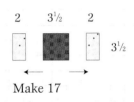

Make 17

2. Sew unit from step 1 between two 2" x 6 1/2" Fabric C pieces as shown. Press. Make seventeen.

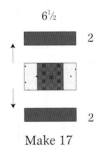

Make 17

3. Sew unit from step 2 between two 2" x 6½" Fabric D pieces as shown. Press. Make seventeen.

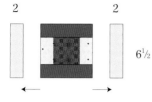

2   2

6½

Make 17

4. Sew unit from step 3 between two 2" x 9½" Fabric E pieces as shown. Press. Make seventeen.

9½

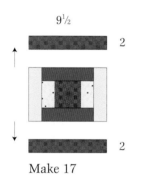

2

2

Make 17

5. Sew unit from step 4 between two 2" x 9½" Fabric F pieces as shown. Press. Make seventeen.

2   2

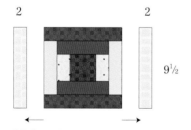

9½

Make 17

6. Sew unit from step 5 between two 2" x 12½" Fabric G pieces as shown. Press. Make seventeen Courthouse Blocks. Block measures 12½" square.

12½

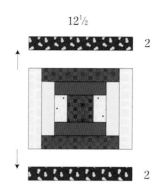

2

2

Make 17
Block measures 12½" square

Block A

1. Refer to Quick Corner Triangles on page 78. Sew two 2½" Fabric C squares to a 2½" x 4½" Fabric B piece as shown. Press. Make forty-eight.

C = 2½ x 2½
B = 2½ x 4½
Make 48

2. Sew a 2½" x 4½" Fabric I piece to unit from step 1 as shown. Press. Make forty-eight.

4½

2½

Make 48

3. Sew a 4½" Fabric C square between two units from step 2 as shown. Press. Make twelve.

4½

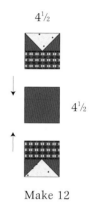

4½

Make 12

4. Draw diagonal line on wrong side of a 5" Fabric B square. Place one Fabric B square and one 5" Fabric C square right sides together. Sew a scant ¼" away from drawn line on both sides to make half-square triangles. Make twenty-four. Cut on drawn line and press toward fabric C. Square to 4½". This will make forty-eight half-square triangles.

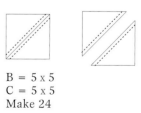

B = 5 x 5
C = 5 x 5
Make 24

Make 48
Square to 4½"

5. Sew one unit from step 2 between two half-square triangles from step 4 as shown. Press. Make twenty-four.

Make 24

6. Sew unit from step 3 between two units from step 5 as shown. Press. Make twelve Block A. Block measures 12½" square.

Block A

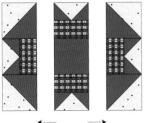

Make 12
Block measures 12½" square

Block B
1. Making quick corner triangle units, sew two 2½" Fabric H squares to a 2½" x 4½" Fabric E piece as shown. Press. Make twenty-four.

H = 2½ x 2½
E = 2½ x 4½
Make 24

2. Sew a 2½" x 4½" Fabric E piece to unit from step 1 as shown. Press. Make twenty-four.

4½

2½

Make 24

3. Sew a 4½" Fabric I square between two units from step 2 as shown. Press. Make six.

4½

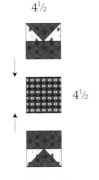

4½

Make 6

4. Draw diagonal line on wrong side of a 5" Fabric H square. Place one Fabric H square and one 5" Fabric E square right sides together. Sew a scant ¼" away from drawn line on both sides to make half-square triangles. Make twelve. Cut on drawn line and press toward Fabric E. Square to 4½". This will make twenty-four half-square triangles.

H = 5 x 5
E = 5 x 5
Make 12

Make 24
Square to 4½"

5. Sew a unit from step 2 between two half-square triangles from step 4 as shown. Press. Make twelve.

Make 12

6. Sew a unit from step 3 between two units from step 5 as shown. Press. Make six Block B.

Block B

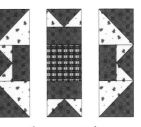

Make 6
Block measures 12½" square

Assembly

1. Refer to photo on page 66 and quilt layout. Arrange and sew blocks in seven horizontal rows of five blocks each, alternating blocks as shown. Press seams in opposite directions from row to row.

2. Sew rows together. Press.

3. Sew 1½"-wide First Border strips end to end to make one continuous 1½"-wide strip. Refer to Adding the Borders on page 80. Measure quilt through center from side to side. Cut two 1½"-wide First Border strips to that measurement. Sew to top and bottom of quilt. Press toward border.

4. Measure quilt through center from top to bottom, including borders just added. Cut two 1½"-wide First Border strips to that measurement. Sew to sides of quilt. Press toward border.

5. Repeat steps 3 and 4 to join, fit, trim, and sew 3½"-wide Second Border and 6½"-wide Outside Border strips to top, bottom, and sides of quilt. Press seams toward border.

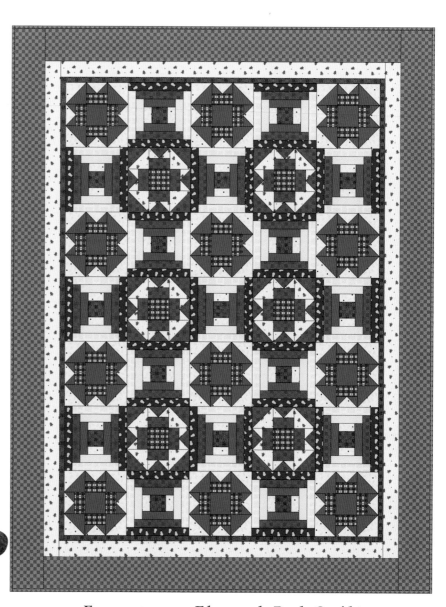

Foursquare Flannel Bed Quilt

Finished Size: 81" x 105"
Photo: page 66

Layering and Finishing

1. Cut backing crosswise into three equal pieces. Sew pieces together to make one (approximate) 90" x 120" piece. Cut backing to 90" x 113". Arrange and baste backing, batting, and top together, referring to Layering the Quilt on page 80.

2. Hand or machine quilt as desired.

3. We used bias strips for our binding. Refer to Making Bias Strips on page 78. Start with a 34" square to cut bias strips. You will need approximately 390" of 2³/4"-wide bias strips. (If you prefer to make a straight cut binding instead of bias, cut ten 2³/4" x 42" strips.) Refer to Binding the Quilt on page 80 and bind quilt to finish.

Foursquare Flannel Pillowcase

Lay your head on this cozy flannel pillowcase and drop off to a dreamland full of warmth and softness! A perfect match for the Foursquare Flannel Quilt, this colorful pillowcase is a snap to sew.

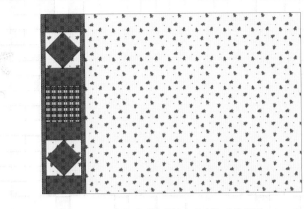

Finished Size: 20" x 30"

Fabric Requirements for One Pillowcase:

Fabric A Pillowcase and Accent Triangles - (1¹/6 yards)
 one 40¹/2" x 25¹/2" piece
 eight 2¹/2" squares
Fabric B Rectangles and Squares - (¹/6 yard)
 two 4¹/2" squares
 four 4¹/2" x 2¹/2" pieces
Fabric C Center Square - (Scrap)
 one 4¹/2" square
Accent Border/Band - (⁵/8 yard)
 one 10¹/2" x 20¹/2" piece
 one 6" x 20¹/2" piece
 one 1" x 20¹/2" piece

Making the Pillow

1. *Refer to Quick Corner Triangles on page 78 to sew four 2¹/2" Fabric A squares to 4¹/2" Fabric B square. Press. Make two.*

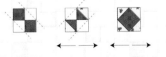

A = 2¹/2 x 2¹/2
B = 4¹/2 x 4¹/2
Make 2

2. *Refer to pillowcase layout to arrange and sew four 4¹/2" x 2¹/2" Fabric B pieces, units from step 1, and one 4¹/2" Fabric C square. Press. Unit measures 4¹/2" x 20¹/2".*

3. *Sew unit from step 2 between 1" x 20¹/2" and 6" x 20¹/2" Accent Border/Band pieces. Press seams toward borders.*

4. *Placing right sides together, sew 10¹/2" x 20¹/2" Accent Border/Band piece to unit from step 3 at 10¹/2" seams to form a tube. Press seams open. Fold tube in half lengthwise, wrong sides together and press. This forms a band for pillowcase.*

5. *Fold 40¹/2" x 25¹/2" Fabric A piece in half crosswise, right sides together, to make a 20¹/4" x 25¹/2" piece. Sew two sides of pillowcase, leaving one 20" side open. Insert unit from step 4 inside Fabric A pillowcase placing pieced side of unit to right side of Fabric A. Pin in place and sew with a ¹/4"-wide seam. Zig zag or serge raw edges of seams to finish. Press and turn right side out.*

Finished Size: 61" x 61"

Snow Crystals
Lap Quilt & Pillow

Reminiscent of a crystalline winter's night, this dazzling display of interlocking snowflakes is guaranteed to draw admiring glances. Only you will know that the complex design is an illusion created by the clever interplay of dark and light fabrics and simple, quick-pieced assembly techniques.

Fabric Requirements and Cutting Instructions

Read all instructions before beginning and use ¼"-wide seam allowances throughout. Read Cutting the Strips and Pieces on page 78 prior to cutting fabrics.

Snow Crystals Lap Quilt and Pillow 61" x 61"	FIRST CUT		SECOND CUT	
	Number of Strips or Pieces	Dimensions	Number of Pieces	Dimensions
Fabric A Background *⅔ yard for each of five fabrics*	2*	3½" x 42"	16*	3½" squares
	2*	2½" x 42"	24*	2½" squares
	6*	1½" x 42"	16*	1½" x 2½"
			32*	1½" x 2"
	**cut for each fabric*		72*	1½" squares
Fabric B Small Snowflake *⅜ yard*	7	1½" x 42"	80	1½" x 2½"
			40	1½" squares
Fabric C Large Snowflake *1 yard* *Makes six blocks*	6	2½" x 42"	48	2½" x 3½"
			24	2½" squares
	8	1½" x 42"	48	1½" x 3½"
			24	1½" x 2½"
			48	1½" squares
	3	1" x 42"	96	1" squares
Fabric D Large Snowflake *⅔ yard* *Makes four blocks*	4	2½" x 42"	32	2½" x 3½"
			16	2½" squares
	6	1½" x 42"	32	1½" x 3½"
			16	1½" x 2½"
			32	1½" squares
	2	1" x 42"	64	1" squares
BORDERS				
First Border *⅓ yard*	5	1½" x 42"		
Second Border *⅓ yard*	6	1½" x 42"		
Outside Border *⅞ yard*	6	4½" x 42"		
Binding *⅝ yard*	7	2¾" x 42"		
Backing - 3¾ yards Batting - 67" x 67" **Cut for each fabric*				

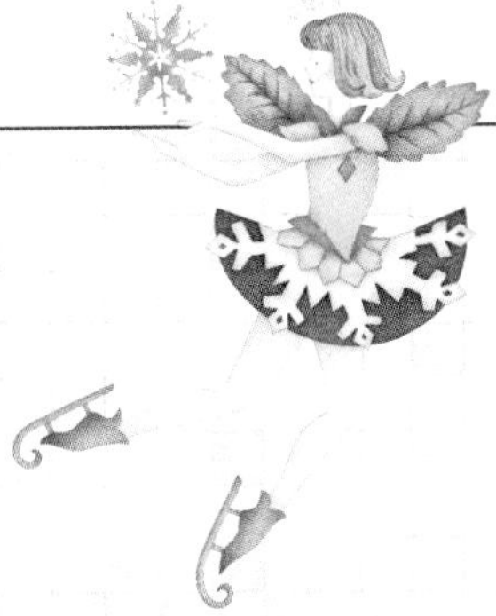

Making the Blocks

You'll be constructing ten Snowflake blocks using five different background fabrics to make a 61" x 61" lap quilt and a 16" square accent pillow. Directions are for two blocks of each color combination. Refer to the quilt layout on page 76, and the color photo to help with fabric placement as you work. Blocks measure 16½" square unfinished. Whenever possible, use the Assembly Line Method on page 78. Press in direction of arrows.

1. Referring to Quick Corner Triangles on page 78, sew two 1½" Fabric A squares to 1½" x 2½" Fabric B piece as shown. Press. Make sixteen.

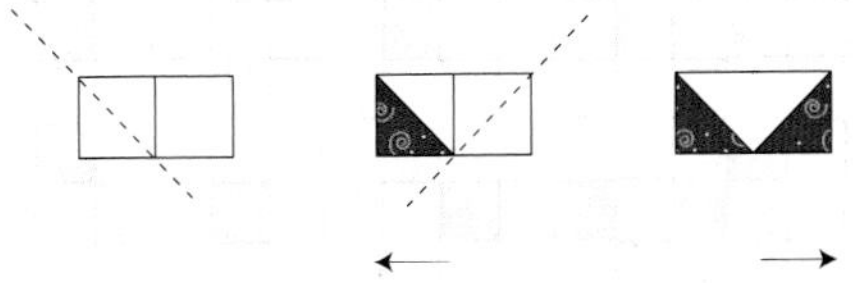

A = 1½ x 1½
B = 1½ x 2½
Make 16

2. Sew 1½" Fabric B square to unit from step 1 as shown. Press. Make eight.

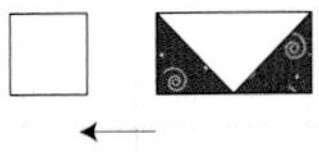

Make 8

3. Sew 2½" Fabric A square to each remaining unit from step 1 as shown. Press. Make eight.

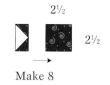

Make 8

4. Sew units from steps 2 and 3 together in pairs as shown. Press. Make eight.

Make 8

5. Making quick corner triangle units, sew 2½" Fabric A square and 1½" Fabric A square to 2½" x 3½" Fabric C piece as shown. Press. Make eight of each variation. One variation will be used in step 6, the remaining units will be used in step 19.

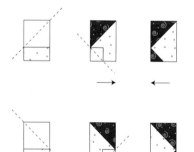

A = 2½ x 2½
     1½ x 1½
C = 2½ x 3½
Make 8 of each variation

6. Sew 3½" Fabric A square to a unit from step 5 as shown. Press. Make eight.

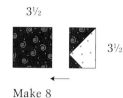

Make 8

7. Sew units from steps 4 and 6 together in pairs as shown. Press. Make eight.

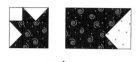

Make 8

8. Making quick corner triangle units, sew two 1½" Fabric A squares to a 2½" Fabric C square as shown. Press. Make eight.

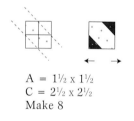

A = 1½ x 1½
C = 2½ x 2½
Make 8

9. Sew 1½" x 2½" Fabric A piece to each unit from step 8. Press. Make eight.

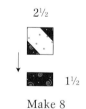

Make 8

10. Sew 3½" Fabric A square to each unit from step 9 as shown. Press. Make eight.

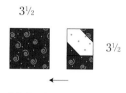

Make 8

11. Making quick corner triangle units, sew 1" Fabric C square to 1½" x 2" Fabric A piece as shown. Press. Make sixteen of each variation.

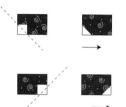

C = 1 x 1
A = 1½ x 2
Make 16 of each variation

12. Sew units from step 11 together in pairs as shown. Press. Make sixteen.

Make 16

13. Sew a unit from step 12 to 1½" x 3½" Fabric C piece as shown. Press. Make sixteen.

Make 16

14. Sew 1½" x 2½" Fabric A pieces and 1½" Fabric C squares together as shown. Press. Make eight.

Make 8

15. Sew units from steps 13 and 14 together as shown. Press. Make eight.

Make 8

16. Sew units from steps 10 and 15 together as shown. Press. Make eight.

Make 8

17. Sew 1½" Fabric A square to 1½" Fabric C square. Press. Make eight.

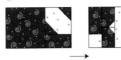

Make 8

18. Sew a 1½" x 2½" Fabric C piece to unit from step 17 as shown. Press. Make eight.

Make 8

19. Sew unit from step 13 between units from steps 5 and 18 as shown. Press. Make eight.

Make 8

20. Sew each unit from step 16 between units from step 7 and step 19. Press. Make eight.

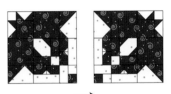

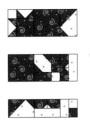

Make 8
Block measures
8½" square

21. Sew units from step 20 together in pairs, taking care to position them as shown. Press. Make four.

Make 4

22. Sew units from step 21 together in pairs, as shown. Press. Make two. Block measures 16½" square.

Make 2
Block measures 16½" square

23. Repeat steps 1-22 to make two blocks of each two remaining A/B/C fabric variations. Make two blocks each of two fabric A/B/D variations to make a total of ten blocks.

Assembly

1. Refer to color photo on page 72 and layout below. Arrange Snowflake blocks in three horizontal rows of three blocks each, randomly placing colors as desired. Sew blocks into horizontal rows. Press seams in every other row in opposite directions. Sew rows together. Press.

2. Sew 1½"-wide First Border strips end to end to make one continuous 1½"-wide strip. Press. Measure quilt through center from side to side. Trim two 1½"-wide First Border strips to that measurement. Sew to top and bottom of quilt. Press seams toward border.

3. Measure quilt through center from top to bottom, including borders just added. Trim two 1½"-wide First Border strips to that measurement. Sew to sides. Press.

4. Repeat steps 2 and 3 to join, fit, trim, and sew 1½"-wide Second Border and 4½"-wide Outside Border to top, bottom, and sides of quilt. Press toward each added border.

Layering and Finishing

1. Cut Backing crosswise into two equal pieces. Sew pieces together to make one 67" x 84" (approximate) backing piece. Cut backing to 67" x 67". Arrange and baste backing, batting, and top together referring to Layering the Quilt on page 80.

2. Hand or machine quilt as desired.

3. Sew 2¾"-wide binding strips end to end to make one continuous 2¾"-wide binding strip. Refer to Binding the Quilt on page 80 and bind quilt to finish.

Snow Crystals Lap Quilt

Finished Size: 61" x 61"
Photo: page 72

Snow Crystals Pillow

Refer to Finishing Pillows on page 80, to layer and quilt top, and sew two 11" x 16½" backing pieces to pillow front. Refer to Pillow Forms page 80 to make a pillow form if desired.

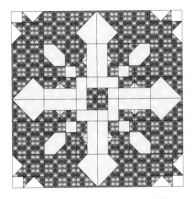

Snow Crystals Pillow

Finished Size: 16" square
Photo: page 72

Northern Lights Pillow

Vibrant flashes of color arch across the dawn sky on this striking pillow top. Waves of light and pattern ripple in the unique border, creating a luminously lovely pillow.

Finished Size: 26½" square

Materials Needed

Fabric A Background - (⅝ yard)
  six 2½" x 6½" pieces
  twenty-eight 2½" squares
  one hundred twelve 1½" squares
Fabric B Light Beams - (assorted scraps)
  cut for each of seven different
  fabrics, five 2½" squares
First Border - (⅙ yard)
  four 1" x 40" strips
*Outside Border - (1⅛ yard cut
lengthwise OR ⅝ yard for
non-directional fabric)*
  four 4¼" x 40" strips
Lining and Batting - (⅞ yard)
  30" square each
Pillow Backing - (⅞ yard)
  two 16¼" x 26½" pieces
Pillow Form - 18"

Making the Pillow

1. *Referring to Quick Corner Triangles on page 78, sew four 1½" Fabric A squares to 2½" Fabric B square. Press. Make four.*

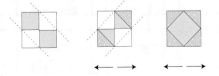

A = 1½ x 1½
B = 2½ x 2½

2. *Sew one unit from step 1 between two 2½" Fabric A squares. Press away from center. Make two.*

3. *Sew a matching 2½" Fabric B square between two units from step 1. Press seams toward center.*

4. *Sew unit from step 3 between two units from step 2. Repeat steps 1 through 4 to make seven variations. Block measures 6½" square.*

5. *Sew 2½" x 6½" Fabric A piece between two blocks from step 4. Press. Sew this unit between two 2½" x 6½" Fabric A pieces. Press. Make two.*

6. *Sew remaining blocks from step 4 together. Press.*

7. *Referring to photo, sew rows together and press.*

8. *Sew one 1" x 40" First Border strip to one 4¼" x 40" Outside Border strip lengthwise. Press. Make four. Referring to Mitered Borders on page 80, sew strip units to pillow top on all four sides, mitering corners. Press.*

9. *Refer to Finishing Pillows on page 80 to layer and quilt top, sew backing to pillow, and make pillow form, if desired. When sewing on the backing piece, we stitched following the curve of the border print and rounded corners for an added effect.*

10. *Stitch between pillow top and First Border to create a flange. Insert 18" pillow form.*

General Directions

Cutting the Strips and Pieces

Before you make each of the projects in this book, pre-wash and press the fabrics. Using a rotary cutter, see-through ruler, and a cutting mat, cut the strips and pieces for the project. If indicated on the Cutting Chart, some will need to be cut again into smaller strips and pieces. Make second cuts in order shown to maximize use of fabric. The approximate width of the fabric is 42". Measurements for all pieces include 1/4"-wide seam allowance unless otherwise indicated. Press in the direction of the arrows.

Assembly Line Method

Whenever possible, use the assembly line method. Position pieces right sides together and line up next to sewing machine. Stitch first unit together, then continue sewing others without breaking threads. When all units are sewn, clip threads to separate. Press in direction of arrows.

Embroidery Stitch Guide

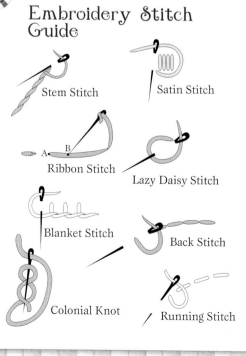

Stem Stitch

Satin Stitch

Ribbon Stitch

Lazy Daisy Stitch

Blanket Stitch

Back Stitch

Colonial Knot

Running Stitch

Quick Corner Triangles

Quick corner triangles are formed by simply sewing fabric squares to other squares or rectangles. The directions and diagrams with each project show you what size pieces to use and where to place squares on corresponding piece. Follow steps 1–3 below to make corner triangle units.

1. With pencil and ruler, draw diagonal line on wrong side of fabric square that will form the triangle. See Diagram A. This will be your sewing line.

A.

sewing line

2. With right sides together, place square on corresponding piece. Matching raw edges, pin in place and sew ON drawn line. Trim off excess fabric leaving 1/4" seam allowance as shown in Diagram B.

B.

trim 1/4" away from sewing line

3. Press seam in direction of arrow as shown in step-by-step project diagram. Measure completed corner triangle unit to ensure the greatest accuracy.

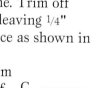

C.

finished corner triangle unit

Making Bias Strips

1. Refer to Fabric Requirements and Cutting Instructions for the amount of fabric required for the specific bias needed.

2. Remove selvages from the fabric piece and cut into a square. Mark edges with straight pin where selvages were removed, as shown. Cut square once diagonally into two equal 45° triangles. (For larger squares, fold square in half diagonally and gently press fold. Open fabric square and cut on fold.)

3. Place pinned edges right sides together and stitch along edge with a 1/4" seam. Press seam open.

4. Using a ruler and rotary cutter, cut bias strips to width specified in quilt directions.

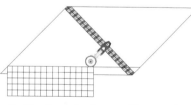

5. Each strip has a diagonal end. To join, place strips perpendicular to each other, right sides together, matching diagonal cut edges and allowing tips of angles to extend approximately 1/4" beyond edges. Sew 1/4"-wide seams. Continue stitching ends together to make the desired length. Press seams open.

6. Cut strips into recommended lengths according to quilt directions.

Quick-Fuse Appliqué

Quick-fuse appliqué is a method of adhering appliqué pieces to a background with fusible web. For quick and easy results, simply quick-fuse appliqué pieces in place. Use sewable, lightweight fusible web for the projects in this book unless indicated otherwise. Finishing raw edges with stitching is desirable. Laundering is not recommended unless edges are finished.

1. With paper side up, lay fusible web over appliqué design. Leaving 1/2" space between pieces, trace all elements of design. Cut around traced pieces, approximately 1/4" outside traced line. See Diagram A.

A.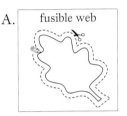
fusible web

2. With paper side up, position and iron fusible web to wrong side of selected fabrics. Follow manufacturer's directions for iron temperature and fusing time. Cut out each piece on traced line. See Diagram B.

B.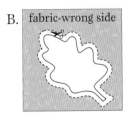
fabric-wrong side

3. Remove paper backing from pieces. A thin film will remain on wrong side of fabric. Position and fuse all pieces of one appliqué design at a time onto background, referring to color photos for placement. Fused design will be the reverse of pattern traced.

Appliqué Pressing Sheet

An appliqué pressing sheet is very helpful when there are many small elements to apply using a quick-fuse appliqué technique. The pressing sheet allows small items to be bonded together before applying them to the background. The sheet is coated with a special material that prevents the fusible web from adhering permanently to the sheet. Follow manufacturer's directions. Remember to let the fabric cool completely before lifting it from the appliqué sheet. If not cooled, the fusible web could remain on the sheet instead of the fabric.

Machine Appliqué

This technique should be used when you are planning to launder quick-fuse projects. Several different stitches can be used: small narrow zigzag stitch, satin stitch, blanket stitch, or another decorative machine stitch. Use an appliqué foot if your machine has one. Use a tear-away stabilizer or water-soluble stabilizer to obtain even stitches and help prevent puckering. Always practice first to adjust your machine settings.

1. Fuse all pieces following Quick-Fuse Appliqué Directions.
2. Cut a piece of stabilizer large enough to extend beyond the area you are stitching. Pin to the wrong side of fabric.
3. Select thread to match appliqué.
4. Following the order that appliqués were positioned, stitch along the edges of each section. Anchor beginning and ending stitches by tying off or stitching in place two or three times.
5. Complete all stitching, then remove stabilizers.

Hand Appliqué

Hand appliqué is easy when you start out with the right supplies. Cotton or machine embroidery thread is easy to work with. Pick a color that matches the appliqué fabric as closely as possible. Use appliqué or silk pins for holding shapes in place, and a long, thin needle, such as a sharp, for stitching.

1. Make a template for every shape in the appliqué design. Use a dotted line to show where pieces overlap.
2. Place template on right side of appliqué fabric. Trace around template.

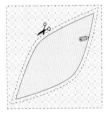

3. Cut out shapes 1/4" beyond traced line.
4. Position shapes on background fabric, referring to quilt layout. Pin shapes in place.
5. When layering and stitching appliqué shapes, always work from background to foreground. Where shapes overlap, do not turn under and stitch edges of bottom pieces. Turn and stitch the edges of the piece on top.
6. Use the traced line as your turn-under guide. Entering from the wrong side of the appliqué shape, bring the needle up on the traced line. Using the tip of the needle, turn under the fabric along the traced line. Using blind stitch, stitch along the folded edge to join the appliqué shape to the background fabric. Turn under and stitch about 1/4" at a time.

Adding the Borders

1. Measure quilt through the center from side to side. Trim two border strips to this measurement. Sew to top and bottom of quilt. Press toward border.

2. Measure quilt through the center from top to bottom, including the border added in step 1. Trim border strips to this measurement. Sew to sides and press. Repeat to add additional borders.

Mitered Borders

1. Cut the border strips as indicated for each quilt.

2. Measure each side of the quilt and mark center with a pin. Fold each border unit crosswise to find its midpoint and mark with a pin. Using the side measurements, measure out from the midpoint and place a pin to show where the edges of the quilt will be.

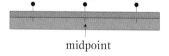

midpoint

3. Align a border unit to quilt. Pin at midpoints and pin-marked ends first, then along entire side, easing to fit if necessary.

4. Sew border to quilt, stopping and starting 1/4" from pinmarked end points. Repeat to sew all four border units to quilt.

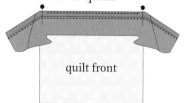

quilt front

5. Fold corner of quilt diagonally, right sides together, matching seams and borders. Place a long ruler along fold line extending across border. Draw a diagonal line across border from fold to edge of border. This is the stitching line. Starting at 1/4" mark, stitch on drawn line. Check for squareness, then trim excess. Press seam open.

fold

back of quilt — stitch — 1/4" — trim

Layering the Quilt

1. Cut backing and batting 4" to 8" larger than quilt top.

2. Lay pressed backing on bottom (right side down), batting in middle, and pressed quilt top (right side up) on top. Make sure everything is centered and that backing and batting are flat. Backing and batting will extend beyond quilt top.

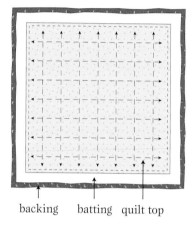

backing   batting   quilt top

3. Begin basting in center and work toward outside edges. Baste vertically and horizontally, forming a 3"– 4" grid. Baste or pin completely around edge of quilt top. Quilt as desired. Remove basting.

Binding the Quilt

1. Trim batting and backing to 1/4" from raw edge of quilt top.

2. Fold and press binding strips in half lengthwise with wrong sides together.

3. Lay binding strips on top and bottom edges of quilt top with raw edges of binding and quilt top aligned. Sew through all layers, 1/4" from quilt edge. Press binding away from quilt top. Trim excess length of binding.

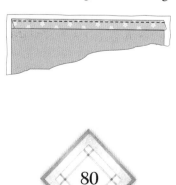

4. Sew remaining two binding strips to quilt sides through all layers including binding just added. Press and trim excess length.

5. Folding top and bottom first, fold binding around to back then repeat with sides. Press and pin in position. Hand stitch binding in place.

← fold top and bottom binding in first

Finishing Pillows

1. Layer batting between pillow top and lining. Baste. Hand or machine quilt as desired, unless otherwise indicated. Trim batting and lining even with raw edge of pillow top.

2. Narrow hem one long edge of each backing piece by folding under 1/4" to wrong side. Press. Fold under 1/4" again to wrong side. Press. Stitch along folded edge.

3. With right sides up, lay one backing piece over second piece so hemmed edges overlap, making single backing panel the same measurement as the pillow top. Baste backing pieces together at top and bottom where they overlap.

Baste

Baste

4. With right sides together, position and pin pillow top to backing. Using 1/4"-wide seam, sew around edges, trim corners, turn right side out, and press.

Pillow Forms

Cut two Pillow Form fabrics to finished size of pillow plus 1/2". Place right sides together, aligning raw edges. Using 1/4"-wide seam, sew around all edges, leaving 4" opening for turning. Trim corners and turn right side out. Stuff to desired fullness with polyester fiberfill and hand-stitch opening closed.